THE MOUNTAIN POEMS OF

THE MOUNTAIN POEMS
OF STONEHOUSE

石屋禪師山居詩

translation and commentary by
RED PINE

Copper Canyon Press
Port Townsend, Washington

Cover art: Tang Yin, *The Thatched Hut of Dreaming of an Immortal,* early
16th-century China, ink and color on paper. H: 29.6. W: 682.1 cm. Courtesy
Freer Gallery of Art, Smithsonian Institution, Washington, D.C.: Purchase,
F1939.60 detail

Grateful acknowledgment is made to Empty Bowl Press for its previous
publication of *The Mountain Poems of Stonehouse.*

Copper Canyon Press is in residence at Fort Worden State Park in Port
Townsend, Washington, under the auspices of Centrum. Centrum is a
gathering place for artists and creative thinkers from around the world,
students of all ages and backgrounds, and audiences seeking extraordinary
cultural enrichment.

LIBRARY OF CONGRESS CATALOGING-IN-PUBLICATION DATA
Qinggong, 1272-1352, author.
[Poems. English]
The Mountain Poems of Stonehouse / Stonehouse [author], Red Pine
[translator].
    pages   cm
ISBN 978-1-55659-455-7 (pbk. : alk. paper)
ISBN 978-1-55659-556-1 (hardback)
1. Qinggong, 1272–1352 — Translations into English. 2. Zen poetry, Chinese —
Translations into English. I. Red Pine, 1943– translator. II. Title.
PL2694.C57A2 2014
895.11'44—dc23

                                                            2013050812

Copper Canyon Press
Post Office Box 271
Port Townsend, Washington 98368

www.coppercanyonpress.org

for Stefan Hyner and Mimi Steele

CONTENTS

If you've never heard of Stonehouse, you're not alone. Not many people have, even in China, even among Buddhists, much less poets. Back in the early 1980s when I was translating the poems of Hanshan (寒山), or Cold Mountain, one of the Chinese editions I was using was published by Taiwan's Hsinwenfeng (新文豐) Publishing Company, and it included the poems of two other Buddhist poets. When I got to the end of Cold Mountain's poems, there was Stonehouse waiting for me. I couldn't believe my good fortune. I was captivated by his poems. And yet I couldn't find anyone in Taiwan who had heard of him. Undeterred, once I finished Cold Mountain's poems, I translated Stonehouse's as well.

Publishing them, though, was a problem. It was hard enough finding a publisher in America for Cold Mountain, who at least had a reputation of sorts. Trying to interest a publisher in Stonehouse was a nonstarter. I ended up publishing his *Mountain Poems* myself in a limited edition distributed by my friends at Empty Bowl in Port Townsend. Although that edition soon went out of print, I later combined it with Stonehouse's other works—his *Gathas* and *Zen Talks*—and published all three in a single volume entitled *The Zen Works of Stonehouse*, first with Mercury House and later with Counterpoint Press. The *Mountain Poems,* though, have remained my favorite, and I have thought about revising my earlier translations and bringing them out again in a separate volume. And now the same press that published my Cold Mountain translations thirty years ago has offered to do just that. So here they are, Stonehouse's *Mountain Poems,* the same poems I translated and published back in 1986. Only now they're better. But first, let me tell you about the poet no one knows about.

-&

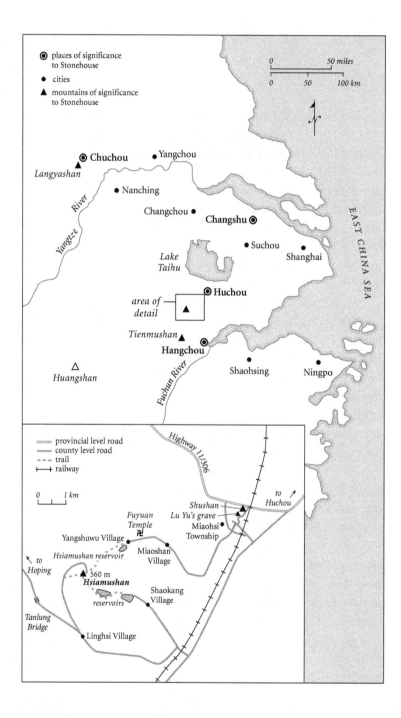

places of significance to Stonehouse

cities

mountains of significance to Stonehouse

0 *50 miles*
0   50   100 km

EAST CHINA SEA

⊙ **Chuchou** • Yangchou
Langyashan ▲

• Nanching

Changchou • **Changshu** ⊙

Lake Taihu • Suchou
Shanghai •

area of detail ⊙ **Huchou** ▲

Tienmushan ▲ ⊙
Hangchou

△ *Huangshan*

Fuchun River

Shaohsing • Ningpo •

provincial level road
county level road
trail
railway

Highway 11/306

0   1 km

Fuyuan Temple 卍
Yangshuwu Village ●
Hsiamushan reservoir
Shushan ▲
Lu Yu's grave Miaohsi Township
Miaoshan Village
to Huchou

↖ *to Hoping*
▲ 560 m
Hsiamushan
reservoirs
Shaokang Village

Tanlung Bridge
● Linghsi Village

Stonehouse was born in 1272 in the town of Changshu (常熟), not far from where the Yangtze empties into the East China Sea. Nothing is known about his family or his early life, other than that his father's surname was Wen (温) and his mother's surname was Liu (劉) and that he received the traditional Confucian education for someone from a family of means. No one knows either when he started using the name Stonehouse (Shihwu, 石屋) or why. He probably picked up the name while he was still studying to become an official. It was the name of a cave on Yushan (虞山), just outside his hometown. Yushan was known for its pine trees, its rock formations, and its springs, in particular a spring that flowed out of a cave as big as a house. Locals still call it Stonehouse Cave. Ironically, the scenes of Yushan were among the favorite subjects of Huang Kung-wang (黃公望, 1269–1354), one of the great artists of the time. Huang was also born in Changshu, and his grave is still there on Yushan, not far from the cave from which Stonehouse took his name. It was not uncommon for an educated person to assume such a name. Many people took several names in the course of their careers, especially artists and poets.

Despite Stonehouse's Confucian upbringing, when he was twenty, he changed tracks. He quit his studies and became a novice under the guidance of Master Yung-wei (永惟) at Hsingchiao Chungfu Temple (興教崇福寺) just outside Changshu. After three years, he was formally ordained and given the monastic name Ch'ing-kung (清珙). Being a young monk, he did what many young monks did back then and still do today: he sought further instruction. One day soon after his ordination, he saw a monk walk past his door wearing a broad-brimmed straw hat—the kind travelers wore to keep the sun out of their eyes and the rain off their shoulders. The monk also had a hiking staff in his hand. When Stonehouse asked where he was going, the monk said he was going to Tienmushan (天目山) to see Kao-feng Yuan-miao (高峰原妙), a great Zen master of the time. He invited Stonehouse to join him, and the two monks journeyed there together. It wasn't far—maybe a four- or five-day journey on foot, assuming they didn't shorten it by availing themselves of the Grand

Canal as far as Hangchou. Kao-feng was living on the West Peak of Tienmushan, just south of Hangchou.

Following their arrival, Kao-feng asked Stonehouse why he had come. Stonehouse said, "I've come for the Dharma." Kao-feng said, "The Dharma isn't so easy to find. You'll need to burn your fingers for incense."[1] To this, Stonehouse replied, "But I see the master before me with my own eyes. How could the Dharma be hidden?" Kao-feng nodded his approval and suggested Stonehouse study the koan "All things come back to one" (萬法歸一).

Stonehouse stayed with Kao-feng for three years, serving with diligence but without satisfying his quest for the Dharma. Stonehouse finally decided to leave and went to announce his departure. Kao-feng said, "You're still a blind donkey. But over in the Huai watershed (淮河), there's a master named Chi-an (及庵). Why don't you go see him?" Stonehouse followed this suggestion. He traveled west to the old capital of Nanching, crossed the Yangtze, and found Chi-an outside Chienyang (建陽)[2] on Langyashan (琅琊山) at West Peak Temple (西峰寺).

Chi-an asked Stonehouse where he came from, and Stonehouse told him, "From Tienmu." Chi-an asked, "And what instruction did you receive?" Stonehouse said, "All things come back to one." When Chi-an asked what that meant, Stonehouse didn't answer. Chi-an said, "Those words are dead. Where did you pick up such rot?" Stonehouse bowed and asked to be instructed. Chi-an said, "Tell me what this means: 'Don't stop where there are buddhas. Hurry past where there aren't any buddhas.'" Stonehouse answered, "I don't understand." Chi-an replied, "More dead words." Stonehouse still didn't understand, but he decided to stay with Chi-an.

Finally, one day Chi-an asked him what the koan about buddhas meant, and Stonehouse answered, "When you mount a horse, you

---

1. This bizarre and extreme practice is rare but still occurs, as evidenced by the monk known as Eight Fingers (八指頭陀), one of the better poet monks of the late nineteenth century.
2. An old name for Chuchou (滁州).

see the road." Chi-an said, "You've been here now for six years. Is that all you've learned?" Exasperated, Stonehouse left. But on his way down the mountain, he looked up and saw a pavilion. Suddenly he understood.[3] He hurried back and told Chi-an, "'Don't stop where there are buddhas.' Those are dead words. 'Hurry past where there aren't any buddhas.' Those are dead words, too. Now I understand living words." Chi-an asked, "And what do you understand?" Stonehouse answered, "When the rain finally stops in late spring, the oriole sings from a tree."[4] Chi-an nodded his approval. Later, when Stonehouse decided to leave, Chi-an told him, "In the future, we will share the same niche."

Not long afterward, Chi-an was asked to take over as abbot of Taochang Temple (道場寺) outside Huchou (湖州), and Stonehouse later joined him there. When Chi-an introduced his disciple to the assembly, he said, "Here is a rare fish that slipped through the net and entered the Dharma Sea." After several years at Taochang Temple, Stonehouse was invited to become the meditation master of Hangchou's famous Lingyin Temple (靈隱寺), a hundred kilometers to the south. It was a prestigious post in the monastic world, but after a short stay Stonehouse decided he preferred the mountains. He traveled back toward Huchou, and twenty-five kilometers south

---

3. Halfway up the trail to the main temple on Langyashan stands Tsuiweng Pavilion (醉翁亭), which still bears the name given to it by Ou-yang Hsiu (歐陽修, 1007–1072) during his tenure as magistrate of Chienyang. It remains the area's most famous sight and was, I presume, the location, if not the source, of Stonehouse's insight into Zen. Its name means Pavilion of the Old Drunkard and is taken from the inscription Ou-yang Hsiu left there in 1046, and which Stonehouse would have known by heart. Many educated people in China still do. It ends, "The birds know the joys of the mountains and forests, but they don't know the joys of the people. And the people know the joys of accompanying the Magistrate on his hikes, but they don't know the joy that their joy gives the Magistrate. He who can share the joy of others while drunk and describe it while sober, this is the Magistrate. And who is the Magistrate? Ou-yang Hsiu of Luling."

4. Confucius said of the oriole, "When it rests, it knows where to rest. Is it possible man is not equal to this bird?" (*Great Learning*: 3.2).

of the city he took up residence at the southern summit of Hsiamu-shan (霞幕山), where he built a hut and began life as a hermit. The year was 1312, and he was forty years old. A contemporary wrote that Stonehouse lived a hard life, refusing to beg for food in nearby villages, unlike other hermit monks. When he ran out of food, he survived on water and wild plants. According to this early account, he was hard on himself but kind and generous to others.

Stonehouse enjoyed the seclusion of the mountain for twenty years, until the spring of 1331. The previous year Emperor Wen had ordered Fuyuan Temple (福原寺) rebuilt in what is now Hsintai County (新埭鎮), eighty kilometers east of Hsiamushan. The temple was originally built in 1312 by the emperor's father, and once the rebuilding was finished, he asked Stonehouse to take over as the temple's abbot. Stonehouse at first declined but was admonished, "If monks are supposed to work for the benefit of the Dharma, how can they succeed while living in idleness and isolation." And so, Stonehouse left Hsiamushan and took up his post as abbot of Fuyuan Temple.[5]

While he was there, he gave instruction in Zen,[6] but his heart remained in the mountains. Finally, after seven years, he pleaded old age, and in 1338 he returned to the mountain. This time, he settled on the mountain's northern summit, known as Hsiawushan (霞霧山). It was toward the end of this second stay, around the year 1350,

---

5. The only source that gives a date for Stonehouse's arrival at this monastery is the prefatory statement by the compiler of Stonehouse's book *Zen Talks*, who lists the fourth month of the Hsinwei (辛未) year, which occurred in 1331. But the same statement also lists the reign period of Yuantung (元統), which didn't begin until 1333. Clearly, one of these dates is wrong. My guess is that 1331 is correct. First, Emperor Wen, who reportedly asked Stonehouse to serve as abbot, died in 1332. Second, the Yuantung period didn't begin until the last month of 1333. Hence, if the Yuantung period were correct, Stonehouse could not have arrived until the fourth month of 1334. But the compiler of the *Zen Talks* also says that upon Stonehouse's arrival, he was appointed administrator of monastic affairs for the entire region, an office that was eliminated in 1334.

6. Stonehouse's *Zen Talks* were compiled by Stonehouse's disciple Chih-jou (至柔), the same disciple who compiled Stonehouse's *Mountain Poems* and *Gathas*. My translations of both texts can be found in *The Zen Works of Stonehouse*.

that he compiled his *Mountain Poems,* which included poems that spanned both periods of residence on the mountain.

Soon afterward, in the spring of 1352, in recognition of his reputation as one of the age's great Dharma masters, the empress presented Stonehouse with a golden robe. His disciples were in awe, but Stonehouse remained unmoved. In autumn of that same year, on the twenty-first day of the seventh moon, he told his disciples he was feeling ill. The following night, he announced he was leaving them. One of them asked whether he had any parting words. Stonehouse picked up his writing brush one last time and wrote:

> Corpses don't stink in the mountains
> there's no need to bury them deep
> I might not have the fire of samadhi
> but enough wood to end this family line[7]

He dropped the brush and died. He was eighty-one. Mindful of Chi-an's premonition that someday both teacher and disciple would share the same niche, Stonehouse's disciples put their teacher's cremated remains next to those of Chi-an, which Stonehouse had already interred on Hsiawushan, not far from where he built his second hut. Three hundred years later, a local official is reported to have opened Stonehouse's stupa while restoring it. The relics emitted such an intense light, the official was dumbfounded and couldn't move. Only after others had re-interred the relics and repaired the stupa did the light stop and the official recover. Earlier, a portion of Stonehouse's relics was sent to the Korean monk Taego Pou (太古普愚),[8] who in turn presented them to his ruler, King Kong-min (恭愍王, r. 1351–74), who had a stupa built for them.

---

7. This poem appears as number 114 in all three Ming dynasty editions of the *Mountain Poems,* but it is not present in more recent editions.

8. Taego first visited China in 1347 and impressed Stonehouse enough that he called him his Dharma heir. Taego is still revered in Korea as the founding patriarch of the Chogye Order (曹溪宗), which united the various schools of Zen in his country and which more recently instigated the first conference ever held in China to discuss Stonehouse's works and contributions.

This then is all I have been able to find out about Stonehouse. It is based largely on Stonehouse's stupa inscription, which was written in the fall of 1377 and which has survived in the three Ming dynasty editions of his poems, while the stupa itself has not.

In the fall of 1991, I decided to see what more I could learn by visiting the mountain on which Stonehouse once lived. I was traveling with my friends Steve Johnson and Finn Wilcox, gathering material for a series of English-language radio programs I later recorded and broadcast on Metro News in Hong Kong, and Huchou was on the way.

In Taiwan I had located Hsiamushan south of Huchou on a declassified Chinese military map. But I had neglected to bring the adjoining sections with me and had no idea how to reach the mountain from Huchou. All I remembered was that it was southwest. I looked at the route map on the Huchou bus station wall and picked Teching (德清), a town about forty kilometers to the south. I reasoned that if we hiked into the mountains west of Teching, sooner or later we would stumble onto Hsiamushan. I went to the ticket window and asked for three seats on the next bus to Teching. Not many foreigners passed through Huchou in 1991, and when the ticket agent saw us, she left and returned with the stationmaster. I told him we wanted three tickets to Teching. He nodded and sold us tickets for a bus due to leave thirty minutes later.

Meanwhile, a crowd of onlookers had gathered, and the stationmaster suggested we would be more comfortable waiting in his office. We gladly accepted. After exchanging introductions, I asked him whether he had ever heard of Hsiamushan. But neither he nor anyone at the station recognized the name. Perhaps the name had changed, I thought. While our host left to get us some tea, I looked around his office. On the wall behind me was a detailed topographic map of the entire county. It took me about thirty seconds to find

Hsiamushan. It actually existed. After six hundred years, the name was still the same, and it was only twenty-five kilometers southwest of Huchou. When the stationmaster returned, we told him to forget Teching, we wanted to go to Hsiamushan, and I pointed to the map. He not only refunded our fares, he went outside to hire a taxi to take us there. While we were waiting, I continued to pore over the map and also located Taochangshan (道場山), which was where Stonehouse lived with Chi-an before moving to Hsiamushan.

A few minutes later, we were in the taxi and on our way there. After heading south about five kilometers, we turned east and drove as far as we could up a rutted dirt road. A muddy trail led us the rest of the way to Wanshou Temple (萬壽寺). In Stonehouse's day it was called Taochang Temple and was considered one of the ten great Zen centers in all of China. But it had since fallen on hard times, very hard times.

Inside the main shrine hall, we met the abbot, Master Fu-hsing (馥馨). He said that during the Cultural Revolution everything was destroyed, except the main hall's T'ang dynasty pillars, a T'ang dynasty well, and the Sung dynasty pagoda on the ridge behind the temple. He invited us to join him for tea and a dessert of fried rice pudding. While we sipped our tea and ate our pudding, I showed him my edition of Stonehouse's poems. I asked him whether he had heard of Stonehouse or Chi-an. He just shook his head. We chatted for half an hour, and as soon as we finished our pudding, we said goodbye. The day was half-gone, and we were anxious to find Hsiamushan while there was still light.

We returned to the highway and continued south. I should have borrowed the stationmaster's map or at least drawn my own and written down the village names along the way. We spent the next hour stopping every few kilometers to ask people along the roadside whether we were headed in the right direction. Everyone shrugged, and we continued on in ignorance. Finally, just after the road crossed a set of railroad tracks, a farmer told us to turn west onto a dirt lane just wide enough for a single car. We followed his directions, and after four or five kilometers we came to a village. It was at the foot of a mountain, and as luck would have it, the villagers called their mountain Hsiamushan.

They pointed us back the way we had come, to a turnoff, which we took up an even narrower track that led along the west side of the mountain. It was slow going, but our driver managed to keep his battered blue Skoda sedan going far beyond where sense would have suggested he stop. The road, such as it was, circled around the north side of the mountain and brought us to just below the summit, where a chain and a compound of blockhouses barred our way. Our driver parked his car, and before anyone inside the buildings had time to come out, we got out and climbed over the chain and started up a trail that led the rest of the way to the top of the mountain.

A few minutes later, we were there, at the summit — not that we had a better view. The bamboo was so high, we couldn't see beyond it. But there was something other than bamboo at the summit. There was a metal tower and a big metal dish and a bunker, from which six soldiers came running with rifles pointed in our direction. As they surrounded us, the base commander came puffing up the trail from one of the blockhouses below. I explained that we were looking for traces of a monk who had lived on the mountain six hundred years earlier — which in China isn't as silly as it sounds. I showed him my string-bound edition of Stonehouse's poems. Along with my translations, it included the Chinese text. His eyes opened wide, and he smiled. He pulled out his machete, waved the soldiers away, and led us straight into the bamboo. It was a variety known as arrow bamboo, which produces the most delicious shoots but which becomes incredibly thick if allowed to grow wild.

The commander and his machete disappeared before us. We tried to follow, but the bamboo was so dense that we sometimes found ourselves stuck, unable to move our arms or our legs. Yet somehow we always got unstuck and managed to find the commander's swath ahead of us. After twenty minutes and maybe two hundred meters, we finally emerged at a small farmstead and open vistas just south of the summit.

The commander said that before the telecommunication base

was built,[9] the farmhouse was the only structure on the mountain. As we approached, a farmer appeared in the doorway and waved for us to come inside. He said the place was originally a small Buddhist temple whose monks had been forced to leave during the Cultural Revolution. In the six hundred years since Stonehouse lived there, the place hadn't changed much. The roof was covered with tiles instead of thatch. And the walls were made of rock instead of bamboo and mud. But the dirt floor was probably the same dirt floor. And the spring Stonehouse called Sky Lake still flowed from the rocks in back. And the slopes were still covered with tea and bamboo. And there were still a couple of pines hanging on.

The farmer poured us tea, and we sat down on the tree stumps he used for chairs. He lived there alone, he said. His children had grown up, and his wife had moved down to the village at the foot of the mountain where life was easier. He had been living at the summit by himself, he said, for the past twenty years. Like Stonehouse, he didn't have much to say. I was reminded of the penultimate verse of the *Mountain Poems*:

I built my hut on top of Hsia Summit
plowing and hoeing make up my day
a half dozen terraced fields
two or three hermit neighbors
I made a pond for the moon
and sell wood to buy grain
an old man with few schemes
now you know everything I own[10]

That was in 1991. Twenty years later, I visited the mountain again in the company of several other foreign friends and a local historian

---

9. I later learned that the buildings, which included both radar and telecommunication facilities, were commissioned in the early 1960s by Lin Piao (林彪), who was Minister of Defense at the time. Their purpose was to help protect Nanching from an air attack by Taiwan.
10. Poem 183.

Yulin Temple

named Wu Zhen (吳震), better known by his *nom de thé*: Dacha (大茶), or Big Tea. We drove up the mountain on a much smoother road this time. It was still dirt, but it was smoother. Just before the summit, we parked at the same place as before. I was surprised to see that the blockhouses had been replaced by a water-bottling plant. And there was no chain to climb over this time. We followed the same old trail again on foot, but it was now wide enough for a car. A few minutes later, the trail ended where I expected to see the old farmhouse. But the farmhouse had become a temple. It was called Yunlinsi (雲林寺), or Cloud Forest Temple. As we approached, we heard chanting. We arrived as the noon chant was ending and just in time for lunch. As the abbot came out of the shrine hall, he saw us and led us into the mess hall, where several dozen laywomen were sitting down to the noon meal, which is always the biggest meal of the day at any Buddhist monastery. The laywomen made room for us at one of the tables, and we enjoyed a memorable lunch of mostly mountain

Site of Stonehouse's first hut on Hsiamushan

produce. The place had changed, but it was still surrounded by hill-sides of bamboo and tea.

Afterward, Big Tea led us back to the bottling plant and just beyond it to the ruins of another farmhouse-temple near the northern part of the summit. He said most scholars were of the opinion that this was where Stonehouse lived, not at Yunlin Temple, which was where I thought he lived. It was so dark and swampy, I was not convinced. But my friends and I had other places to go that day, and we didn't linger.

Recently, I visited the mountain again, again with Big Tea. I had some questions only another walk around the top of the mountain could answer, including questions concerning the location of Stonehouse's hut. Was it at Yunlin Temple, or was it near the water-bottling plant? Since my previous visit, Big Tea had found some old maps of the mountain, maps that were part of the Huchou Gazetteer (湖州地方志) published back in the nineteenth century. I was

Distant view of Hsiamushan from vicinity of Fuyuan Temple

surprised to see that the summit of the mountain had two names.
The southern part of the summit was labeled Hsiamushan, and
the northern part was labeled Hsiawushan. Stonehouse used both
names in his poems, but no one had given any thought to what that
meant. Most likely they thought it was a printing error or reflected
a change in the mountain's name whereby both names were at one
point retained. But seeing both names on the same mountain, I came
to a different conclusion, namely, that Stonehouse lived in two dif-
ferent places on the same mountain.

In poem 170, Stonehouse says he moved to Hsiamushan in 1312,
not to Hsiawushan, while his stupa inscription, composed in 1377,
lists his residence as being on Hsiawushan, not on Hsiamushan.
Rather than confusing the issue of where Stonehouse lived, the idea
of two locations made sense. After all, Stonehouse vacated his first
hut on Hsiamushan when he became abbot of Fuyuan Temple in
1331. When he did, another hermit most likely moved in. I'd seen

that happen in China on other mountains where hermits lived. So when Stonehouse returned in 1338, he chose a new location for his hut, near what was now the water-bottling plant, where he noted in one of his last poems: "who would have guessed at seventy-seven / I would dig a pond for lotus roots and water chestnuts."[11] Clearly, he was not living at Sky Lake anymore, the name he gave to the spring-fed pond near his first hut.

Walking around both locations only helped confirm this, as I began seeing certain poems in one of the two locations but not in the other. Finally, I felt I had cleared up the confusion about the location of Stonehouse's residence, at least to my satisfaction. As for Stonehouse's stupa and the stupa of his teacher, they were some-where in the ruins of the stupa cemetery whose nameless stones cov-ered the overgrown slope near Stonehouse's second hut. One of the stupas was still intact, but it dated back only to the Ch'ing dynasty. A Korean Buddhist group also visited the mountain, and in 2008 they erected a memorial stupa to commemorate Stonehouse's trans-mission of the Dharma to Korea. But Stonehouse's own stupa had merged with the hillside.

In my earlier edition of these poems I neglected to mention their textual basis. When I first translated the *Mountain Poems*, I was liv-ing at Bamboo Lake (竹子湖), a farming village near the summit of Chihsingshan (七星山) an hour by bus north of Taipei. But my wife was still living with her parents in the city, and their apartment was only a five-minute walk from Taiwan's National Central Library. One day when I was in town and had nothing better to do, I decided to see what I could find in the library's archives. I should have vis-ited earlier. Within a matter of minutes, I found three Ming dynasty copies of Stonehouse's poems. Surprisingly, two of these early cop-ies were published only a few decades after Stonehouse's death. One

---

11. Poem 24.

copy included a preface written at Hangchou's Lingyin Temple by the poet-monk Yu-chang Lai-fu (豫章來復) and dated the fifteenth year of the Hungwu (洪武) reign period, or 1382. A second copy was less precise and listed only the Hungwu period (1368–1398) as its date of publication. The third copy was published near the end of the Ming dynasty in 1615 by P'an Shih-jen (潘是仁). Naturally, a number of later editions of the *Mountain Poems* have appeared over the years. But I have based my translations on these three early copies, and where variants occur, I have invariably sided with the Ming dynasty versions and have mentioned this in my notes.

Since I first translated and published Stonehouse's *Mountain Poems*, I have moved on to other poets. But Stonehouse is still my favorite, and whenever I give a public reading, I invariably include a few of his poems. But I have discovered that I can't read just any poem. Many of my earlier translations, I have found, don't read that well. This, I presume, is a problem every translator of poetry encounters. What I translate one day doesn't read that well the next. And this goes on, until the publisher says it's time to send in the manuscript. Hence, reading my translations years later, I cannot help but cringe. Some translations still work. Others don't. Of course, translators know that translating poetry is not the same as translating prose, that when you translate a poem you have to make a poem. But a translator doesn't work the same way as a poet. A translator has to go through a different process to bring a poem from one language into another. I don't know how others do it, but when I've tried to think of a metaphor for what I go through, I keep coming up with the image of a dance. I see the poet dancing, but dancing to music I can't hear. Still, I'm sufficiently enthralled by the beauty of the dance that I want to join the poet. And so I try. And as I do, I try not to step on my partner's feet (the so-called literal or accurate translation), but I also try not to dance across the room (the impressionistic translation or version — usually by someone who doesn't know the poet's language). I try to get close enough to feel the poet's rhythm, not only the rhythm of the words but also the rhythm of the poet's heart. And I love Stonehouse's heart. So I've hit the dance floor one more time. I like to think I've become better at this over the years. But just as there is no perfect dance, there is no perfect translation. It can always be better. But not today. Today it feels perfect. Just don't ask me tomorrow.

I've also decided to separate Stonehouse's *Mountain Poems* from his *Gathas* and *Zen Talks* and to publish them separately, as I first did in 1986. The reason is that poems need room on the dance floor. I wasn't able to do that when I combined all three of Stonehouse's surviving texts in *The Zen Works of Stonehouse,* where as many as seven poems appeared on a page. But I'm fortunate to have found a publisher willing to indulge me. So here they are again, Stonehouse's *Mountain Poems,* all dressed up and ready to go. If they have fallen into your hands, surely the muses have smiled upon you. Say hello to your new best friend.

Red Pine
April 10, 2013
Port Townsend, Washington

THE MOUNTAIN POEMS OF STONEHOUSE

余山林多暇瞌睡之餘偶成偈語自娛。紙墨少便不欲紀之。雲衲禪人請書蓋欲知我山中趣向。於是靜思隨意走筆不覺盈帙故掩而歸之。復囑慎勿以此為歌詠之助當須參意則有激焉。

Here in the woods I have lots of free time. When I don't spend it sleeping, I enjoy composing poems. But with paper and ink so scarce, I haven't thought about writing them down. Now some Zen monks have asked me to record what I find of interest on this mountain. I have sat here quietly and let my brush fly. Suddenly this volume is full. I close it and send it back down with the admonition not to try singing these poems. Only if you sit on them will they do you any good.

吾家住在雪溪西
水滿天湖月滿溪
未到盡驚山險峻
曾來方識路高低
蝸涎素壁粘枯殼
虎過新蹄印雨泥
閒閉柴門春晝永
青桐花發畫胡啼

柴門雖設未嘗關
閒看幽禽自往還
尺壁易求千丈石
黃金難買一生閒
雪消曉嶂聞寒瀑
葉落秋林見遠山
古栢煙消清晝永
是非不到白雲間

1. Both the East and the West Forks of the Tiao River (苕溪) originate in the Tienmu Mountains west of Hangchou, meet in Huchou, then flow into nearby Lake Taihu. The last stretch of their combined waters, from Huchou to Taihu, is called the Cha River. As early as the Sung dynasty, the city of Huchou was also referred to by this name. Hence, when Stonehouse says he lived west of Cha River, he means west of Huchou. Actually, the mountain on which he lived was twenty-five kilometers to the southwest. Sky Lake was the name he gave to the small pond in front of his hut. Nowadays, it is also called Butterfly Spring (蝴蝶泉), because of the shape of its two "wings," or Medicine Spring (葯泉), because of the reputed healing quality of its water. Until recently, hermits in China often reported encounters with the South China tiger, which is much smaller than its Siberian and Bengali cousins but still dangerous. The paulownia is one of China's most fragrant trees. It blooms in late March and early April and is the only tree on which the phoenix will alight—should a phoenix be flying by. In the last line, I've read hua-hu (畫胡), a compound not attested in any dictionary or database, as a copyist error or local usage for hua-mei (畫眉): "thrush."

2. The fourth-century Buddhist monk Chih Tun (支遁) became the butt of jokes when he tried to buy a mountain from the hermit who lived on it (cf. A New Account of Tales of the World: 25.18).

SEVEN-SYLLABLE VERSES

1   I made my home west of Cha River
where water fills Sky Lake and the moon fills the stream
strangers are frightened by the mountain's heights
but once they arrive they know the trail
dried snail shells on rock walls
fresh tiger tracks in the mud
I leave my door open when spring days get longer
when paulownias bloom and thrushes call

2   To glimpse the fluttering of shy birds
I don't always close the door I made
a piece of jade is worth more than a cliff
but gold can't buy a lifetime of freedom
the sound of icy falls on a dawn-lit snowy ridge
the sight of distant peaks through leafless autumn woods
mist lifts from ancient cedars and clear days last forever
right and wrong aren't found in the clouds

荒塚纍纍沒野蒿　昔人未葬盡金腰
有求莫若無求好　進步何如退步高
貪餌金鱗終落釜　出籠靈翮便冲霄
山翁不管紅塵事　自種青麻織布袍

紙窗竹屋槿籬笆　客到蒿湯便當茶
多見清貧長快樂　少聞濁富不驕奢
看經移案就明月　供佛簪瓶折野花
盡說上方兜率好　如何及得老僧家

3. Gold seals were the prerogative of royalty and high-ranking officials. The graves of the elite of the preceding Southern Sung dynasty were located east of the capital of Hangchou near the city of Shaohsing. With the fall of the Southern Sung, they were abandoned to weeds and later desecrated in 1278 by the Mongols, who dug up more than a hundred royal graves and pillaged the surrounding area following their conquest of the southern half of China.

4. The paper used for windowpanes was treated with oil to make it waterproof. The hibiscus is often used to form hedges in the warmer southern half of China. The first line becomes two lines in poem 62. Wormwood, which includes several varieties of *Artemisia,* is used as a general tonic and specifically as an antipyretic and in chronic dysentery. A tea or soup is made from leaves and buds picked before the plant flowers in summer. It was once common to drink such a soup on the fifth day of the fifth moon, or Poet's Day, which commemorates the death of the poet Ch'u Yuan (屈原, d. 278 BC). Hermits tend to go to bed when the sun goes down, but not on moonlit nights. Tushita is the name of the highest heaven in the realm of desire and is where bodhisattvas reside before their final rebirth, when they become buddhas.

3   Grave upon grave buried beneath weeds
     before their funerals they carried gold seals
     but desire is no match for detachment
     and how can ambition compete with restraint
     lured by bait golden fish end up in kettles
     uncaged magic wings fly high
     worldly affairs don't concern a hermit
     I weave my robe from homegrown hemp

4   A paper-window bamboo hut a hedge of hibiscus
     wormwood soup for tea when guests arrive
     the poor people I meet are mostly content
     rare is the rich man not vain or wasteful
     I move my table to read sutras by moonlight
     I pick wildflowers to fill my altar vase
     everyone says Tushita Heaven is fine
     but how can it match this place of mine

道在人弘孰可憑　發言須與行相應
貪心似海何時足　妄念如苗逐日增
幾樹梅花清處士　一園芋子樂閒僧
而今隨例菴居者　見道忘山似不曾

動則乖真靜則差　非思量處更淆訛
無心未合祖師意　有念盡為煩惱魔
矮屋朝陽寒氣少　疎籬種菊晚香多
白雲曳曳方拖練　又被風吹過綠蘿

5. Confucius said, "A man can glorify the Way. The Way does not glorify a man" (*Analects*: 15.28). When Tzu-chang asked how he should act, Confucius replied, "To your words be true, in your deeds be sincere" (*Analects*: 15.5). The plum blossom's association with purity and seclusion was immortalized in the poems of Lin Ho-ching (林和靖, 967–1028), a recluse who lived on a small island in Hangchou's West Lake. More than one Zen master has summarized their Buddhist path in words similar to those of Ch'ing-yuan Hsing-ssu (青原行思), a disciple of Hui-neng: "Thirty years ago, before I began practicing Zen, I saw mountains as simply mountains. Then, while I was practicing Zen, I realized mountains were not mountains. But now that I understand Zen, I see mountains are simply mountains" (*Wutenghuiyuan*: 17).

6. Movement is the practice of mortals, and stillness is the practice of Hinayana monks. Bodhidharma says, "While ordinary people keep giving birth to the mind, claiming it exists, disciples of the Hinayana keep wiping out the mind, claiming it doesn't exist. But bodhisattvas and buddhas neither create nor annihilate the mind" (*The Zen Teaching of Bodhidharma*: p. 53). The Indian Patriarch of Zen is often pictured meditating while facing a wall, while T'ao Yuan-ming, the poet of recluses, is said to have entered samadhi while picking chrysanthemums along his fence. Clouds are often used as metaphors for thoughts, while vines represent convoluted logic. Drifting clouds can also refer to wandering monks.

5   To glorify the Way what should people turn to
to words and deeds that agree
but oceans of greed never fill up
and sprouts of delusion keep growing
plum trees in bloom cleanse a recluse
a garden of taro cheers a lone monk
those who follow rules in their huts
never see the Way past the mountains

6   Movement isn't right and stillness is wrong
and cultivating no-thought means confusion instead
the Patriarch didn't have no-mind in mind
any thought at all means trouble
a hut facing south isn't so cold
chrysanthemums along a fence perfume the dusk
as soon as a drifting cloud starts to linger
the wind blows it past the vines

松下雙扉冷不扃　一龕金像照青燈
眠雲野鹿驚回夢　落澗獼猴墜折藤
得意看山山轉好　無心合道道相應
多時不向門前去　蘚葉苔花積幾層

二十餘年住崦西　钁頭邊事不吾欺
一園春色熟茶笋　數樹秋風老栗梨
山頂月明長嘯夜　水邊雲暖獨行時
舊交多在名場裏　竹戶長開待阿誰

7. The first couplet suggests a small mountain shrine and the faint flame of an oil lamp.

8. According to the *Shanhaiching* (Western Mountains: 4), China's oldest book of geography, the sun sets behind Mount Yen at the westernmost reaches of the empire. To live west of Mount Yen was to live in the wilderness. The realm of Amita Buddha was also said to be west of the setting sun, the contemplation of which constitutes the first of sixteen visualizations once used in Pure Land meditation. In China, the best tea is usually picked in late March or early April. The same is true for bamboo shoots. The term Stonehouse uses here, *ch'ang-hsiao* (長嘯), and which I translate as "drone," refers to something akin to throat singing. It was once cultivated by Taoists as a breathing technique to generate *ch'i* (氣). In ancient times, many poets had their designated *hsiao-t'ai* (嘯台), or droning platforms, just for that purpose. Civil service exams were discontinued in North China during most of the Yuan dynasty, but they were still held periodically in the provincial capital of Hangchou, which was only sixty kilometers south of Hsiamushan. Before he became a monk, Stonehouse also spent a good deal of his youth studying for exams. See also poem 20. In the first line, "twenty years" suggests this poem was written near the end of Stonehouse's first stay on the mountain, which, in fact, lasted twenty years. Altogether, he spent thirty-four years on the mountain.

7　　Below the pines its twin doors are never closed
　　　its gilt statue is lit by blue light
　　　a monkey breaks a vine and falls into a stream
　　　startled deer resume their dreams in the clouds
　　　glad to see mountains I like mountains better
　　　the Way finds me without me trying
　　　it's been so long since I went to the gate
　　　the lichen and moss must be inches thick

8　　More than twenty years west of Mount Yen
　　　I've never been cheated by a hoe
　　　a garden in spring of new tea and bamboo
　　　a few trees in fall of ripe chestnuts and pears
　　　I drone on the summit when the moon is bright
　　　and walk along the stream when the clouds turn warm
　　　with so many friends in examination halls
　　　why do I leave my door open

翠寶丹崖列四傍　茅菴恰好在中央
一身布衲衣裳煖　百念消融歲月忘
石瘦種來蒲葉細　土深迸出筍茅長
有時夜半聞鐘磬　知有招提在下方

莫謂山居便自由　年無一日不懷憂
竹邊婆子常偷筍　麥裏兒童故放牛
栗蟥地蠶傷菜甲　野猪山鼠食禾頭
施為便有不如意　只得消歸自己休

9. A monk's robe is traditionally made of twenty-five patches, one for each of the twenty-five kinds of existence and the twenty-five kinds of understanding that liberate its wearer from such existence. The rushes (most likely *Juncus effusus*) were for mats and meditation cushions. The large bell in a Buddhist temple is normally rung around four o'clock in the morning and again around nine o'clock at night. But beginning in the Sung dynasty, temple bells were also rung at midnight to remind people of the Buddha's teaching of impermanence. The temple to which Stonehouse is referring was most likely Fuyuan Temple (福原寺), at the northeast foot of Hsiamushan near Yangshuwu Village (楊樹塢). Among the temple's extensive overgrown ruins, a stone slab with Stonehouse's name on it was recently unearthed, attesting to some sort of association with the place. Stonehouse probably spent time there before moving to the summit, and at some point he was probably the temple's abbot as well, even if in name only. However, this Fuyuan Temple is not to be confused with the temple of the same name outside Pinghu where Stonehouse served as abbot at the emperor's request.

10. Elders and children are often assigned the more marginal tasks in a farm family, such as gathering medicinal herbs or wild plants in the hills and grazing the family ox or water buffalo.

9   Green gullies and red cliffs wherever I look
     and my thatch hut in between
     beneath a patched robe my body stays warm
     I've forgotten my worries along with the date
     rushes grow thin where the soil is rocky
     bamboo shoots grow tall where it's deep
     sometimes at midnight I hear a bell
     and remember there's a temple down below

10   Don't think a mountain home means you're free
     a day doesn't pass without its cares
     old ladies steal my bamboo shoots
     boys lead oxen into the wheat
     grubs and beetles destroy my greens
     boars and squirrels devour the rice
     things don't always go my way
     what can I do but turn to myself

菴住霞峰最上頭　　巖崿巉嶮少人遊
擔柴出市青苔滑　　負米登山白汗流
口體無厭宜節儉　　光陰有限莫貪求
老僧不是閒忉怛　　只要諸人放下休

嘯月眠雲二十年　　自憐衰老見時艱
烏來索飯生臺立　　僧去化粮空鉢還
鰕蜆人爭撈白水　　钁鉏我且斸青山
黃精食盡松花在　　不着閒愁方寸間

11. Stonehouse abbreviates the mountain's name here. The word *hsia* (red) refers to the color of clouds at sunrise or sunset and is also used to describe cliffs.

12. According to his contemporaries, Stonehouse preferred not to beg for his food. But he was joined on the mountain by other monks who did. Nearby Lake Taihu is still famous for its tiny white shrimp and freshwater clams. The root of Solomon's seal, or *Polygonatum cirrhifolium,* contains a significant amount of starch. It is usually dug up in early spring. Pine pollen is slightly sweet and also has nutritional value. It is gathered in late spring by placing a sheet under a pine tree and knocking the branches with a bamboo pole. The "square inch" refers to the mind.

11   My hut is at the top of Hsia Summit
      few visitors brave the cliffs and ravines
      lugging firewood to market I slip on the moss
      hauling rice back up I drip with sweat
      with no end to desire less is better
      with limited time why be greedy
      this old monk doesn't mean to cause trouble
      he just wants people to let go

12   After twenty years of nights beneath the moon and the clouds
      to find myself old is hard
      crows come looking for food at the altar
      monks return with empty begging bowls
      others work the waves for shrimp and clams
      I swing a hoe in the mountains
      when Solomon's seal is gone there is still pine pollen
      and one square inch free of care

幽居自與世相分　苔厚林深草木薫
山色雨晴常得見　市聲朝暮罕曾聞
爇茶瓦竈燒黃葉　補衲巖臺剪白雲
人壽希逢年滿百　利名何苦競趨奔

入得山來便學呆　尋常有口懶能開
他非莫與他分辨　自過應須自剪裁
瓦竈通紅茶已熟　紙窗生白月初來
古今誰解輕浮世　獨許嚴陵坐釣臺

13. According to the biography of the ninth-century poet-recluse Lu Kuei-meng (陸龜蒙), as recorded in the *Hsintangshu* (New History of the T'ang Dynasty), Lu never went anywhere without his small portable tea stove, which he felt was among the necessary possessions of every recluse.

14. Lao-tzu said, "Those who seek learning gain every day / those who seek the Way lose every day" (*Taoteching*: 48). Lao-tzu also said, "Everyone has a goal / I alone am dumb and backward" (ibid.: 20). During the preceding Sung dynasty, tea aficionados began boiling their tea instead of steeping it, as they now do. And they often used a small, portable clay stove for that purpose. Yen Tzu-ling and Liu Hsiu (劉秀) were boyhood friends. When Liu led a rebellion that resulted in the restoration of the Han dynasty with himself as Emperor Kuang-wu (光武), he invited his old friend to join him at court. But Yen Tzu-ling declined, preferring the life of a recluse on the Fuchun River (富春江) south of Hangchou, where he spent his days fishing from a boulder. The boulder has since been submerged by the waters of a dam, but the site still bears the name of this famous recluse.

13   Seclusion of course means far from the world
thick moss deep woods and perfumed plants
the sight of mountains rain or shine
no sounds of a market day or night
I burn dry leaves in my stove to make tea
and to patch my old robe I cut a cloud by the cliff
lifetimes seldom fill a hundred years
why suffer chasing profit and fame

14   I entered the mountains and learned to be dumb
I'm usually too tired to open my mouth
I don't point out the mistakes of others
my own faults are what I try to alter
the tea must be ready my clay stove is red
the moon must be up the paper windows are white
who in the past saw through this transient world
Yen Tzu-ling fished alone from his rock

溪淺泉清見石沙　屋頭無角寄藤蘿
夜深月下長猿嘯　苔厚巖前少客過
庭竹欹斜春雪重　嶺梅消瘦夜寒多
寥寥此道非今古　徒把甄來石上磨

15. Stonehouse's hut had no gables because his roof was round, as he tells us in poem 145. I imagine something like a thatched yurt with bamboo walls and a layer or two of mud on the exterior. Gibbons and their eerie howls were once common throughout the Yangtze watershed but are now found in the wild only in a few nature reserves in the extreme south. Huai-jang (懷讓) was the dharma heir of Hui-neng, Zen's Sixth Patriarch. After Hui-neng's death in 713, Huai-jang moved to Fuyen Temple (福嚴寺) on Hengshan (衡山) in southern Hunan province. One day on the slope above the temple, he saw a young monk meditating and asked what he was doing. The young monk said he was trying to become a buddha. Huai-jang picked up a brick and started grinding it on a boulder. When the young monk asked what he was doing, Huai-jang said he was making a mirror. The boulder was still there when I visited in 1991, just up the trail from Huai-jang's grave, but has since disappeared during a road-widening project. The young monk eventually became the Zen master known as Ma-tsu (馬祖). The story was recorded in the *Chuantenglu* (Transmission of the Lamp: 5).

15 The streams are so clear and shallow I can see pebbles
my gableless hut is surrounded by vines
gibbons howl at night when the moon goes down
few visitors get past the moss by the cliffs
the bamboos in my yard bend with spring snow
the plum trees on the ridge are withered by frigid nights
the solitude of this path isn't something new
but grinding a brick on a rock is a waste

白髮禪翁久住菴　衲衣風捲破襤縿
溪邊掃葉供爐竈　霜後苦荳覆橘柑
本有天真非造化　現成公案不須叅
豁開戶牖當軒坐　盡日看山不下簾

16. The Yangtze watershed is the earliest known home of not only the orange but also such citrus fruits as the tangerine, the kumquat, and the pomelo. Apparently Stonehouse's orange tree (or "trees," as Chinese is ambiguous when it comes to number) didn't make it. He never mentions it again. Hermits with the good fortune to inherit such trees from previous residents, or with the patience to wait for saplings to mature, receive enough income when the trees bear fruit to support themselves for several months every year. In North China, hermits receive the same benefit from walnut trees. The Buddhist definition of reality is that which is self-existent and thus dependent neither in time nor in space upon anything else. During the preceding Sung dynasty, enigmatic statements of previous Zen masters were compiled into books and used as subjects (Chinese: kung-an [公案]; Japanese: koan) for meditation and aids to enlightenment. However, by Stonehouse's time, some Zen masters began to view such devices as more likely to become obstacles than aids and moved on to tea.

16   A white-haired Zen monk with a hut for my home
the wind has torn my robe into rags
down by the stream I rake leaves for my stove
after a frost I wrap a mat around my orange tree
ultimate reality isn't created
ready-made koans aren't worth a thought
all day I sit by my open window
looking at mountains without lowering the shade

臥雲深處不朝天　只在重巖野水邊
竹榻夢回窓有月　砂鍋粥熟竈無煙
萬緣歇盡非除遣　一性圓明本自然
湛若虛空常不動　任他滄海變桑田

嶽頂禪房枕石臺　白雲飛去又飛來
門前瀑布懸空落　屋後山巒起浪堆
素壁淡描三世佛　瓦瓶香浸一枝梅
下方田地雖平坦　難及山家無點埃

17. Hermits in the Yangtze watershed and those farther south usually sleep on beds whose sleeping surface consists of woven bamboo or a network of rope, while their colleagues in the colder Yellow River watershed to the north prefer brick beds with built-in ovens. According to Buddhists, only what is not subject to causation, only what is not connected to anything else, is real. Over the past five thousand years, the silt of the Yellow River has formed most of North China out of what used to be the Pohai Sea. So in China the sea did, in fact, turn into mulberry groves.

18. The buddha portraits would most likely have been those of Amita, Shakyamuni, and Maitreya, buddhas of past, present, and future dispensations of the Dharma.

17 I sleep in the clouds where the sun doesn't shine
    beside a high cliff and a mountain stream
    I dream on my cot until the moon fills the window
    the porridge is done when the stove smoke clears
    a million reasons vanish without being driven off
    our single perfect nature shines by itself
    as clear as a cloudless sky it never changes
    the sea meanwhile is now a mulberry grove

18 My Zen hut rests upon rocks at the summit
    clouds fly past and more clouds arrive
    a waterfall hangs in space beyond the door
    a mountain ridge rises like a wave in back
    I drew three buddhas on a wall
    I put a plum branch in a jar for incense
    the fields down below might be level
    but can't match a mountain's freedom from dust

大道從來無盛衰　未明大道著便宜
聖賢隱伏當斯世　邪法流行在此時
痛策諸根休自縱　常存正念莫他為
人身一失袈裟下　萬劫千生不復追

破屋蕭蕭枕石臺　柴門白日為誰開
名塲成隊挨身入　古路無人跨脚來
深夜雪寒唯火伴　五更霜冷有猿哀
袈裟零落難縫補　收捲雲霞自剪裁

19. Buddhists view liberation as freedom from rebirth. No matter how propitious a given life might be, such existence is still a delusion. The Buddhist robe of twenty-five patches protects its wearer from twenty-five kinds of existence in the realms of desire, form, and formlessness that make up the Wheel of Rebirth.

20. Admission to the civil service or military officer corps was based on a series of competitive examinations held at the local, at the provincial, and at the national levels. The examination hall for the region in which Stonehouse lived was in nearby Hangchou. See also poem 8. The patches that make up a monk's robe can consist in anything from hemp to silk or, here, something even less substantial.

19   The Great Way has never known abundance or want
      those who don't see it choose profit instead
      sages and wise men hide from the world
      where counterfeit truth prevails
      rein in your senses and stop indulging
      be ever mindful and nothing else
      once your body disappears beneath a robe
      say goodbye to a thousand rebirths

20   My broken-down hut rests upon rocks
      why do I leave my door open all day
      people who file into exam halls
      don't set foot on an ancient trail
      snow-filled nights a fire is my lone companion
      frost-covered dawns I hear a gibbon howl
      my tattered monk's robe isn't easy to mend
      I cut a new patch when a cloud rolls in

本源自性天真佛　古鏡未磨含眾像　等閒放下便無事　綠霧紅霞竹徑深　　寥寥世道非今昔　流俗沙門真可惜　危如茅草郎當屋　人壽相分一百年

非色非空非古今　洪鐘纔扣發圓音　著意看來還有心　一菴終日冷沉沉　　日把柴門緊閉關　貪名師德更堪憐　險似風波破漏舡　有誰能得百年全

21. In ancient China and India, people believed that the human lifespan once extended for thousands of years and that the limit of one hundred was recent and due to the degeneration of human morals. Buddhists say it is much easier to become enlightened as a monk or a nun than as a layperson beset with the cares and responsibilities of secular life. Hence, to waste such an opportunity on mediocrity or vanity is tragic, indeed.

22. Bamboo grows so thick on Hsiamushan, trails don't last long. When I first visited the mountain in 1991, the army officer who led me to the area where Stonehouse first lived needed a machete to reach it. Until fairly recently, mirrors in China were made of bronze or brass, and they had to be polished in order to reflect. Bodhidharma says, "To find a buddha all you have to do is see your nature. Your nature is the buddha" (*The Zen Teaching of Bodhidharma*: p. 13). In the *Heart Sutra*, Avalokiteshvara says, "Form is emptiness, and emptiness is form." Buddhists often speak of three buddhas: past, present, and future.

21   A human life lasts one hundred years
but which of us gets them all
precarious as a hut made of thatch
or a leaking boat in a storm
mediocre monks are pathetic
would-be masters are sadder still
the world's empty ways aren't new
some days I shut my old door tight

22   A trail through green mist red clouds and bamboo
to a hut that stays cold and dark all day
simply let go and worries end
stop to think and cares reappear
an unpolished mirror holds countless shapes
a great bell resounds only when it is rung
our original nature is the one true buddha
not form or emptiness not past or present

優游靜坐野僧家　飲啄隨緣度歲華
翠竹黃花閒意思　白雲流水淡生涯
石頭莫認山中虎　弓影休疑盞裏蛇
林下不知塵世事　夕陽長見送歸鴉

滿頭白髮瘦稜層　日用生涯事事能
木白秋分春白术　竹筐春半曬朱藤
黃精就買山前客　紫菜長需海外僧
誰道新年七十七　開池栽藕種菱菱

23. Stonehouse traced his spiritual ancestry through his teacher, Chi-an, to the Tiger Hill Zen lineage. The hill, which is in Suchou, was said to resemble a tiger. In his biography in the *Chinshu* (43), Yueh Kuang (樂廣) explains to a distraught guest that the image of a snake in his wine bowl is merely the reflection from a nearby painting. The last two lines recall a line from "West Garden": "In the woods fading rays call the crows home," a poem by Lu You (陸游).

24. The roots of wild thistle, or *Atractylis ovata,* are used as a tonic, especially for the spleen and the stomach. The vine flowers were most likely wisteria racemes, which remain a delicacy of this region and are usually stir-fried. In poem 12, Stonehouse implies that Solomon's seal was readily available on Hsiamushan. Apparently he ate all he could find and was forced to buy more. The seaweed was probably a present from Yu T'ai-ku (Korean: Taego Pou [太古普愚]), who visited Stonehouse the summer of 1347, when Stonehouse was seventy-seven. For more on their meeting and later exchange of letters, see J.C. Cleary's *Buddha from Korea.* Since Stonehouse died at the age of eighty-one and wrote this poem four years earlier, he apparently did not finish his *Mountain Poems* until shortly before his death. Lotus roots and water chestnuts are both nutritious starches that flourish in the watery regions of the Yangtze watershed. Clearly, Stonehouse was doing more than surviving and was even enjoying the occasional indulgence afforded by mountain living.

23   A monk on his own sits quiet and relaxed
        he survives all year on what karma brings
        bamboo and yellow flowers simplify his thoughts
        his life is as plain as a cloud or a stream
        he doesn't mistake a rock for a tiger on a hill
        or the image of a bow for a snake in his bowl
        oblivious in the woods to worldly affairs
        at sunset he watches the crows flying back

24   I may be white-haired and nothing but bones
        but I'm versed in the work of daily survival
        in fall I pound thistles in a wooden mortar
        in spring I dry vine buds in a wicker tray
        I buy Solomon's seal from a peddler down below
        for seaweed I rely on a monk from across the sea
        but who would have guessed at seventy-seven
        I would dig a pond for lotus roots and water chestnuts

卜得重巖遠市朝　柴門半掩草蕭蕭
是誰白髮貧無諂　那箇朱門富不驕
急債莫於寬裏做　妄情須是靜中消
白雲也道青山好　夜夜飛來伴寂寥

風牆來往塞官塘　站馬如飛日夜忙
冒寵貪榮謀仕宦　貪生重利作經商
人間富貴一時樂　地獄辛酸萬劫長
古往今來無藥治　如何不早去修行

25. The first line recalls the opening of Cold Mountain's first poem: "Towering cliffs were the home I chose / bird trails beyond human tracks."

26. The regions north and south of the Yangtze delta are still major producers of salt and silk in China. For many centuries, taxes on these two products provided the central government with its major source of revenue, and trade was tightly controlled, with distribution taking place via the Grand Canal and the Yangtze. The government also maintained an extensive network of horse-mounted couriers for transmission of documents. Buddhists recognize a series of hells in which the length of one's residence is determined by one's karma. A kalpa is a unit of time equivalent to the existence of a world, from its creation until its destruction. The reference to elixir was aimed at Taoist alchemists and their clients, who sought to cheat death through the ingestion of various minerals and herbs. The injunction of the last line suggests Stonehouse must have been reading the poems of Cold Mountain or Pickup the day he wrote this, as both were given to dispensing similar advice.

25   I chose high cliffs far from a market
a half-closed gate overgrown with weeds
where is the pauper who isn't deferential
or the rich man who isn't vain
emergency loans don't come without strings
delusions require stillness to end
clouds too say mountains are better
returning at night they ease the solitude

26   Their zigzagging sails crowd government quays
their relay mounts fly night and day
officials seeking favor and glory
merchants after comfort and gain
but the joys of worldly riches are brief
while the sufferings of hell last ten thousand kalpas
and no elixir has ever been found
better change your ways while you can

入此門來學此宗　切須仔細要推窮
清虛體寂理猶在　忖度心亡境自空
樹掛殘雲成片白　山街落日半邊紅
是風動耶是幡動　不是幡兮不是風

客愛幽閒到竹籬　逢迎應恕禮全虧
滿頭白髮鬢鬆聚　一頂袈裟撩亂披
黃葉火殘終夜後　青猿聲斷五更時
擁衾相對蒲團坐　各自忘言契此機

27. The "gate" is the gate of Zen, and the teaching is Bodhidharma's: "This mind is the buddha" (*The Zen Teaching of Bodhidharma*: p. 9). The last couplet comes from this story: One day two monks were arguing in a temple courtyard. Pointing to a flag flapping in the wind, one said it was the wind that was moving. The other said it was the flag that was moving. Having just arrived at the temple and overhearing their argument, the Sixth Patriarch said, "It isn't the wind that's moving, and it isn't the flag. It's your minds that are moving" (*The Platform Sutra*: p. 123).

28. Given the ambiguity of Chinese grammar, it is unclear whether the white hair and monk robe should be singular or plural. I've decided in favor of the former and that Stonehouse's visitor is a Taoist priest, as Taoist priests, unlike Buddhist monks, don't cut their hair. The leaves suggest Stonehouse used up whatever firewood he had on hand in the course of the night. Meditation cushions were made of woven grass and filled with rice straw, while quilts usually included an inner layer of cotton wadding.

27   Who enters this gate who studies this teaching
has to be thorough and push to the end
still the empty body and reason remains
forget the thinking mind and the world disappears
cloud-draped trees form a landscape of white
the summit turns red as it bites the setting sun
the flag moves or is it the wind
it isn't the wind or the flag

28   A friend of seclusion arrives at my gate
we greet and pardon our lack of decorum
a mane of white hair more or less tied
a monk robe gathered loosely around
embers of leaves at the end of the night
howl of a gibbon announcing the dawn
sitting on cushions wrapped in quilts
words forgotten finally we meet

百歲光陰過隙駒　幾人於此審思惟
己躬下事未明白　生死岸頭真嶮巇
衲定線行嬌婦淚　飯香玉粒老農脂
莫言施受無因果　因在果成終有時

自入山來萬慮澄　平懷一種任騰騰
庭前樹色秋來減　檻外泉聲雨後增
挑薺煮茶延野客　買盆移菊送鄰僧
錦衣玉食公卿子　不及山僧有此情

29. In ancient China, a man was required to have his parents' permission to become a monk. Of course, such a requirement was often ignored, but his wife's approval was not necessary, since she and their children lived with the man's parents. For all their self-reliance, many hermits would starve without the generosity of farmers, many of whom still share their "fat" with them. Alms and acts of charity are likened to seeds planted in a field of blessing, bringing benefit to both the giver and the recipient.

30. Stonehouse did not have the mountain to himself. In fact, during the last decade of his life a number of disciples moved to the summit and built their own huts nearby. The small temple that later developed from where he built his first hut was vacated during the Cultural Revolution but was recently replaced by a new set of buildings and named Yunlin Temple. The small temple that replaced his second hut is still in ruins. Flowering in autumn, chrysanthemums are a symbol of old age. Hospitality to strangers and generosity to friends remain among the virtues cultivated by Chinese of all classes. The gentry included the propertied and educated elites.

29   A hundred years pass by in a flash
how many think this through
if what you're doing right now isn't clear
the edge between life and death is sheer
stitches on a monk's robe are a loving wife's tears
jade grains of rice are an old farmer's fat
don't think who gives receives no reward
a fruit forms in time where there is a seed

30   I entered the mountains and my cares became clear
serene at heart I let them all go
the trees beyond my yard thin out in fall
the stream before my door becomes louder when it rains
I pick greens and boil tea when a fellow hermit arrives
I give a neighbor monk chrysanthemums in a pot from town
the gentry might have their fine food and clothes
but they can't match a mountain monk with scenes like these

自覺從前世念輕　　是身壽命若浮漚
芒鞋竹杖春三月　　事欲稱情常不足
求佛求仙全妄想　　衰榮可喻花開落
松風昨夜熾然說　　我已久忘塵世念

老來任運樂閒情　　只好挨排過了休
紙帳梅花夢五更　　人能退步便無憂
無憂無慮即修行　　聚散還同雲去留
自是聾人不肯聽　　頹然終日倚岑樓

31. The *Diamond Sutra* ends with this gatha: "As a lamp, a cataract, a star in space / an illusion, a dewdrop, a bubble / a dream, a cloud, a flash of lightning / view all created things like this."

32. Shoes made of braided grass or rushes were still worn by farmers in China until fairly recently. The third line is indebted to Su Tung-p'o (蘇東坡): "With rope shoes and a new bamboo staff / I set off on a hundred-coin journey," which in his day would have been enough for a few days at most. The "paper curtains" here refer to a kind of mosquito net that was hung over the bed during Stonehouse's day. It had a gauze top for ventilation and paper sides printed with butterflies and plum blossoms. While Buddhists seek to become buddhas, Taoists seek to become immortals. The fifth-century Taoist T'ao Hung-ching (陶弘景) planted hundreds of pines around his hermitage in Hangchou in order to hear the wind in their branches. The pine wind can also refer to the sound of a buddha's voice.

31   This body lasts about as long as a bubble
       may as well let it go
       things don't often go as we wish
       who can step back doesn't worry
       we blossom and fade like flowers
       we gather and part like clouds
       I stopped thinking about the world a long time ago
       relaxing all day in a teetering hut

32   I saw through my worldly concerns of the past
       I welcome old age and enjoy being free
       rope shoes a bamboo staff the last month of spring
       paper curtains plum blossoms and daybreak dreams
       immortality and buddhahood are merely fantasies
       freedom from worry and care is my practice
       last night what the pine wind roared
       that was a language the deaf can't hear

逐日挨排過了休　明朝何必預先憂
死生老病難期約　富貴功名不久留
湖上朱門縈蔓草　澗邊遊徑變荒丘
所言皆是目前事　只是無人肯轉頭

白髮頭陁老病侵　住來茅屋幾年深
消磨本有凡情執　析蕩今從聖量心
百鳥不來山寂寂　萬松長在碧沉沉
分明空却那邊事　一道神光自古今

33. Buddhism's four afflictions are birth, illness, old age, and death. The lake-side villas would be those along the shore of nearby Lake Taihu. The promenades, I imagine, were along the waters of the Tiao River, whose East and West Forks merged just south of Huchou and flowed through town as the Cha River before entering Taihu.

34. Stonehouse's expression *sheng-liang-hsin* in the fourth line is a contraction of two phrases that occur frequently in the *Lankavatara Sutra,* namely, *sheng-chih* (buddha knowledge) and *liang-hsin* (nothing but mind). The kalpa of nothingness lasts from the destruction of one universe until the creation of the next. Thus, the light Stonehouse sees is from the end of the last universe — such is the power of karma. In Zen, this and other phrases refer to one's original face, one's face before one was born.

33 Day after day I let things go
   why worry about tomorrow today
   the four afflictions are hard to predict
   wealth and honor don't last
   lakeside villas swallowed by vines
   deserted promenades along the river
   these are things anyone can see
   but no one is willing to consider

34 A white-haired monk afflicted with age
   living under thatch year after year
   I've spent my existence on the simplest of passions
   all of which come from the buddha mind
   the mountain is quiet when the birds don't come
   ten thousand pines keep it dark green
   from the kalpa of nothingness it's clear
   a miraculous light still shines

競利奔名何足誇
清閒獨許野僧家

心田不長無明草
覺苑長開智慧花

黃土坡邊多蕨笋
青苔地上少塵沙

我年三十餘來此
幾度晴窗暎落霞

我本禪宗不會禪
甘休林下度餘年

鶉衣百結通身掛
竹篾三條裹肚纏

山色溪光明祖意
鳥啼花笑悟機緣

有時獨上臺盤石
午夜無雲月一天

35. Delusion is one of the three poisons, which also include anger and desire. Fiddlehead ferns made up the diet of two of China's most famous recluses, Po-yi (伯夷) and Shu-ch'i (叔齊, ca. 1100 BC), both of whom preferred to die of hunger rather than eat the produce of a realm ruled by an unfilial king. In characterizing the decades of life, the Chinese often quote Confucius: "Thirty and on one's own. Forty and no doubts" (*Analects*: 2.4). According to poem 170, Stonehouse was forty when he moved to Hsiamushan. However, some local historians of Huchou think he first spent time at Fuyuan Temple northeast of the mountain before moving to the summit. I'm more of the opinion that the temple was built at the beginning of his second stay on the mountain, by disciples who followed him there after he moved out of the much larger temple of the same name a two-day walk to the east.

36. Bodhidharma is usually listed as the First Patriarch of Zen in China, as he was credited with bringing this teaching to China in the late fifth century. However, the traditional beginning of Zen is said to have occurred nine hundred years earlier when the Buddha held up a flower and a monk named Kashyapa smiled. As evidence of his own understanding, Stonehouse told his master, "When the rain finally stops in late spring, the oriole sings from a tree." The flat-topped rock is still there, just up the slope from the water-bottling plant. Local farmers call it "chess-playing rock."

35   Profit and fame aren't worth extolling
     to an untroubled solitary mountain monk
     weeds of delusion don't grow in the mind
     where flowers of wisdom bloom instead
     bamboo shoots and fiddleheads blanket the slopes
     dust seldom falls on moss-covered ground
     I was over thirty when I first arrived
     how many sunsets have turned my windows red

36   I was a Zen monk who didn't know Zen
     so I chose the woods for the years I had left
     a robe made of patches over my body
     a belt of bamboo around my waist
     mountains and streams explain the Patriarch's meaning
     flower smiles and birdsongs reveal the hidden key
     sometimes I sit on a flat-topped rock
     late cloudless nights once a month

四十餘年獨隱居　不知塵世幾榮枯
夜爐助暖燒松葉　午鉢充饑摘野蔬
坐石看雲閒意思　朝陽補衲靜工夫
有人問我西來意　盡把家私說向渠

薑尾狼心滿世間　爭先各自使機關
百年能得幾回笑　一日曾無頃刻閒
車覆有誰知改轍　禍來無地著羞慚
老僧不是多饒舌　要與諸人揭蓋纏

37. Stonehouse lived as a hermit on Hsiamushan for thirty-four years. But he also lived for three years with Kao-feng on the West Peak of Tienmushan and for six years with Chi-an on Langyashan outside Chuchou. Although the Buddhist practice of eating one meal a day was never as widespread in China as it was in India, the noon meal was, and still is, considered the major meal of the day for monks and nuns. "Why did Bodhidharma come from the West?" ("the West" being India) is one of the most popular koans used in Zen meditation. In the last line, the term *chia-ssu* means "patrimony," or "inherited possessions." If there is no self, how can there be possessions? Then again, where would Stonehouse be without his bowl and his robe and his little tea stove? Still, I've never seen a hermit yard sale.

38. One of the first measures enacted by the First Emperor when he unified China in 221 BC was to standardize the axle length of carts so that all tracks would be the same width. As a result, the speed of overland travel was greatly improved. The five blinders (五蓋) or hindrances are desire, anger, sloth, anxiety, and doubt. And the ten chains (十纏) are shamelessness, insensitivity, envy, meanness, regret, laziness, overactivity, self-absorption, hate, and secretiveness.

37   I've lived as a hermit more than forty years
oblivious to the world's ups and downs
a stove full of pine needles keeps me warm at night
a bowl of wild plants fills me up at noon
I sit on rocks and watch clouds and think idle thoughts
I patch my robe in sunshine and cultivate silence
if someone asks why Bodhidharma came from the West
I tell them everything I own

38   Scorpion tails and wolf hearts pervade the world
everyone has a trick to get ahead
but how many smiles in a lifetime
or moments of peace in a day
who can change tracks when their cart tips over
when disaster strikes there's no time for shame
this old monk isn't merely pointing fingers
he's trying to remove people's blinders and chains

烏兔奔忙不蹔停　巖居忽爾到頹齡
水邊行道影加瘦　松下看山眸轉青
紅葉旋收供瓦竈　黃花時採插銅瓶
勞生好飲利名酒　昏醉無由喚得醒

茅屋青山綠水邊　往來年久自相便
數株紅白桃李樹　一片青黃菜麥田
竹榻夜移聽雨坐　紙窗晴啟看雲眠
人生無出清閒好　得到清閒豈偶然

39. According to Chinese mythology, the moon is yin and represents Earth. Hence, its symbol is an animal of the land. And the sun is yang and represents Heaven. Hence, its totem is a creature of the air. Stonehouse's "blue eyes" could allude to the "blue-eyed barbarian," Bodhidharma, who brought Zen to China. But they could also refer to cataracts. Ironically, cataract surgery was introduced to the Chinese by Indian monks about the same time that Bodhidharma arrived, but the technique had been lost by Stonehouse's time. While Stonehouse used chrysanthemums for his altar, others infused them in wine.

39 The crow and the hare race without rest
    living among cliffs I'm suddenly old
    my reflection looks thin when I walk beside a stream
    my eyes have turned blue viewing mountains through pines
    I gather red leaves to fill my tea stove
    I pick yellow flowers for my altar vase
    working for the wine of profit and fame
    others get drunk and can't be revived

40 A thatch hut in blue mountains beside a green stream
    after so many years visits are now up to me
    a few peach and plum trees blooming red and white
    a green and yellow field of vegetables and wheat
    all night I sit in bed listening to rain
    when it clears I open the window and doze off watching clouds
    nothing in life is better than being free
    but getting free isn't luck

古人為道入山中　日用工夫在己躬
添石墜腰舂白米　攜鉏帶雨種青松
擔泥拽石何妨道　運水搬柴好用功
躭懶借衣求食者　莫來相伴老禪翁

萬物生成感宿根　己長彼短不須論
一團猛火利名路　三尺寒氷佛祖門
草莽荊榛狐窟宅　雲霄蓬島鶴乾坤
滿頭白髮居巖谷　幾度凭欄到日曛

41. Traditionally, Buddhist monasteries in China depended on donations from lay believers. And such donations were sometimes in the form of land, the rent from which paid for those things the monks needed. As a result of such rent income, some monasteries became so rich that the monks did little or no work. This was not the case at monasteries in the mountains, where the monastic rules of Pai Chang (百丈清規) prevailed, chief of which was "No work, no food."

42. In this case, "roots" refer to past actions whose karmic fruit we reap today. When Taoist adepts finally succeed in transforming themselves into pure spirit through yoga and alchemy, they are said to fly off as cranes or be carried by cranes to the island of Penglai (蓬萊), the home of immortals. The last couplet suggests Stonehouse wished he had a few more visitors.

41   The ancients entered mountains in search of the Way
their daily practice revolved around their bodies
tying heavy stones to their waists to hull rice
shouldering hoes in the rain to plant pines
moving dirt and rocks it goes without saying
carrying firewood and water they stayed busy
the slackers who put on a robe to get food
don't come to join an old Zen monk

42   Everything's growth depends on its roots
why argue about which is tall or short
the road to fame and fortune is a circle of fire
the door to buddhahood is a wall of ice
my hut sits alone among brambles and weeds
the cloud-wrapped isle of Penglai is a crane's universe
here in the mountains my hair has turned white
I've leaned at the windowsill so often until dark

巖居我本為修行　不許人知每自評
道性淳和餘習盡　覺心圓淨照功成
種松鉏菜一身健　補衲翻經兩眼明
世異事殊真好笑　避秦亦得隱山名

歷遍乾坤沒處尋　偶然得住此山林
茅菴高插雲霄碧　蘚逕斜過竹樹深
人為利名驚寵辱　我因禪寂老光陰
蒼松怪石無人識　猶更將心去覓心

43. In T'ao Yuan-ming's story "Peach Blossom Spring," a group of people flee-
ing the oppressive rule of the Ch'in dynasty (221–207 BC) discovers a hidden
valley. When several centuries later a fisherman stumbles upon their sanctuary,
he finds a peaceful farming community. Eventually, the fisherman returns to
his own village and tells others about his discovery. But the descendants of the
original refugees obliterate the traces he left to mark the way there, and their
hidden valley was never found again.

44. The Chinese have always had a passion for old pine trees and oddly shaped
rocks. In the last line, Stonehouse recalls the Zen monk who sees beyond the
mountains but who has not yet seen beyond the emptiness with which he has
replaced them.

43   I live in the mountains in order to practice
       I don't need others to examine my faults
       when life becomes simple old habits end
       when the mind becomes clear its light finally shines
       planting pines and tilling fields have strengthened my body
       reading sutras and mending clothes have sharpened my sight
       the world's absurdities are absurd indeed
       the refugees of Ch'in are called hermits too

44   I searched high and low without success
       by chance I found this forested peak
       my thatch hut pokes through the clouds and sky
       a moss-covered trail cuts through the bamboo
       the greedy are worried about favor and shame
       I spend my time in the stillness of meditation
       bizarre rocks and gnarled pines remain unknown
       to those who look for the mind with the mind

年老心閒身亦閒　掃除一榻臥松間
巖扃幽寂自為喜　世路崎嶇人轉頑
風暖野禽聲瑣碎　日斜花藥影闌珊
藜羹粟飯家常有　不用持盂更下山

清晨汲水啟柴門　看見天空四斂氛
黃獨火香思嬾瓚　碧桃花謝悟靈雲
林間猿鶴慣曾見　世上衰榮杳不聞
幾度坐來苔石暖　好山直看到斜曛

45. Lines five and six are inspired by Ou-yang Hsiu's *Liuyishihhua,* except that Ou-yang Hsiu has the sun high and the shadows heavy. The term *hua-yao* (cerulean) was used in Stonehouse's time in reference to a certain kind of blue found in the pottery glazes of the preceding Sung dynasty. The leaves of pigweed, or *Chenopodium album,* are eaten fresh as salad greens in Europe but are usually cooked in China. Pigweed has been a metaphor for simple fare ever since Confucius had nothing but this to eat for ten days while traveling through an inhospitable region. Although monks all have a large bowl they use for begging, the hermits I've met coming down the trail invariably carry an empty sack and leave their bowls at home. Stonehouse was known for his refusal to beg for food.

46. The T'ang dynasty official Li Mi heard about Lazy Scrap (Lan-ts'an) and decided to pay him a visit. When Li arrived, Lazy Scrap offered the official part of a yam he was roasting and advised him, "Don't talk too much, and you'll last ten years as prime minister" (*Kaosengchuan*). Li did, in fact, later become prime minister, but his readiness to criticize put him in and out of favor. Magic Cloud (Ling-yun) was enlightened while watching peach petals falling, after which he composed this gatha: "For thirty years I expected a sword / scattering leaves I cut through branch after branch / but since I discovered peach blossoms / I haven't had any more doubts" (*Wutenghuiyuan*: 4).

45   Old but at peace in body and mind
     I cleared a place to rest in the pines
     a remote mountain hut makes me happy
     up-and-down roads make others perverse
     wild birds chatter when the wind turns warm
     cerulean shadows fade as the sun declines
     with pigweed soup and coarse rice at home
     why take my bowl down the mountain anymore

46   Opening my door at dawn to fetch water
     I examine the sky's seasonal moods
     the smell of roasting yams recalls Lazy Scrap
     peach petals falling woke up Magic Cloud
     I usually see gibbons and cranes in the forest
     I hear no news of the world's ups and downs
     I often spend days warming moss-covered rocks
     gazing at the mountains I love until sunset

白雲深處結茅廬　隨分生涯樂有餘
未死且留煨芋火　息機何必絕交書
湛然凝寂通三際　廓爾圓明裏十虛
菴內不知菴外事　幾番花落又還敷

細把浮生物理推　輸贏難定一盤碁
僧居青嶂閒方好　人在紅塵老不知
風颭茶烟浮竹榻　水流花瓣落青池
如何三萬六千日　不放身心靜片時

47. Lines five and six recapitulate the two stages of meditation known as *chih-kuan* (止觀): "stilling" thoughts and "illuminating" what is real.

48. The Chinese play two kinds of chess: *wei-ch'i* (圍棋), which the Japanese call Go, and *hsiang-ch'i* (象棋), which is similar to Indian or Western chess. Both have been played in China for more than three thousand years. In Buddhist parlance, "dust" refers to the world as perceived by the senses. The tea smoke is from the small clay brazier Stonehouse used for boiling tea.

47   I built a thatched hut deep in the clouds
I find enough joy in what life brings
I bury a few potatoes before the fire dies
I'm done with schemes but not with writing letters
clear and still as ice I transcend the bounds of time
open and full of light I encompass the ten directions
but events outside my hut are a mystery to me
like how many times have flowers fallen and bloomed again

48   Examine the patterns of transient existence
the outcome of a game of chess isn't fixed
a monk in the mountains needs to be free
people in the dust grow old unaware
windblown tea smoke floats above my bed
stream-borne petals fill the pond outside
with thirty-six thousand days
why not spend a few staying still

恁麼徹底恁麼去　放下從頭放下來
兩片唇皮堆白醭　一條古路長蒼苔
雲邊木馬飛如電　海底泥牛吼似雷
雪覆萬峯晴月夜　暗香春信到寒梅

清貧長樂道人家　日用頭頭自偶諧
昨夜西風吹古木　天明滿地是乾柴
霞飄素練粘丹壁　露滴真珠綴綠崿
活計從來隨現定　不勞辛苦去安排

49. The third and fourth lines refer to people who talk about the truth without knowing it for themselves. The fifth and sixth lines summarize koans in which the wooden horse that flashes through the clouds and the clay ox that thunders beneath the waves represent the liberated mind free of feelings and thoughts. As to the second of these metaphors, Tung-shan (東山) once asked Lung-shan (龍山) what he had learned while living in the mountains. Lung-shan answered, "I saw two clay oxen plunge into the sea. And since then, I haven't heard any news" (*Chuantenglu*: 8). The last two lines recall a famous couplet about plum blossoms by Lin Ho-ching (967–1028): "Their hidden scent rides the wind / the moon shines through the mist."

50. Buddhists and Confucians also used the word *Tao*, or Way, to describe their path of spiritual and moral practice. The west wind blows in autumn in China and is usually the mildest of the seasonal breezes.

49   To get to the end the very end
       let it all go let it go
       foam piles up on a pair of lips
       moss grows thick on an ancient road
       a wooden horse flashes through the clouds
       a clay ox thunders beneath the waves
       a clear moonlit night amid ten thousand snowy peaks
       a hidden scent says spring has reached the winter plum

50   I'm a poor but happy follower of the Way
       whatever happens takes care of my needs
       last night the west wind blew down an old tree
       at daybreak firewood covered the ground
       windblown white silk wreathed the red scarps
       dewdrop pearls adorned the green cliffs
       my survival has always depended on what's present
       why should I tire myself out making plans

了了常知似不知　翛然如兀又如癡
旋乾倒嶽鎮長靜　一念萬年終不移
有耳聽聲風過樹　無心應物月臨池
休言我獨能明了　此事人人盡可為

計拙慳癙應世才　聰明無分占癡呆
自言境物皆虛幻　誰解資財盡倘來
黃葉隨流閒去住　白雲橫谷謾徘徊
雙眸合却方繞好　為愛青山又放開

52. Confucius said, "The wise love water. The kind love mountains" (*Analects*: 6.21). While wisdom is the basis of enlightenment, compassion is the basis of liberation. The saying of Zen master Ch'ing-yuan Hsing-ssu comes to mind: "Thirty years ago, before I began practicing Zen, I saw mountains as simply mountains. Then, while I was practicing Zen, I realized mountains were not mountains. But now that I understand Zen, I see mountains are simply mountains" (*Wutenghuiyuan*: 17).

51   You know very well yet seem not to know
speechless like a dunce or a fool
you keep still while storms flatten mountains
not a thought moving for ten thousand years
with ears you hear the wind in the trees
with no-mind you respond like a pond to the moon
but don't think you alone understand
this is something anyone can do

52   The shame of dumb ideas is suffered by the best
but the absence of intelligence means a fool for sure
claiming external things are nothing but illusions
yet not understanding wealth is simply luck
the leaves in the stream move without a plan
the clouds in the valley drift without design
I closed my eyes and everything was fine
I opened them again because I love mountains

圓顱方服作沙門　便是牟尼佛子孫
止惡防非調意馬　忘機息見制心猿
鍊磨道性真金淨　涵養靈源美玉溫
把手牽他行不得　惟人自肯乃方親

紅日東升夜落西　黃昏鐘了五更鷄
乾坤老我一頭雪　歲月消磨百甕虀
借地栽松將作棟　喫桃吐核又成蹊
寄言世上傷弓羽　好向深山擇木棲

53. Although Shakyamuni Buddha didn't cut his hair, his disciples began the custom of shaving their heads to distinguish themselves from members of other sects. They also wore the simplest possible garment patched together from rags. In regard to the residents of a Zen monastery, Stonehouse treats slouches and fanatics with equal disdain.

54. The Chinese often eat pickles with their meals, especially the morning meal. For those, such as hermits, who don't have much else, pickled vegetables are often the main course at meals during the winter. The *Chankuotse* (戰國策) says, "When a bird that has been previously shot at hears a bow string, it flies away as fast as it can" (Chutse).

53   A round head and square robe constitute a monk
behold a descendant of Shakyamuni Buddha
stopping wrongs and evils taming the galloping will
banishing schemes and views controlling the monkey mind
refining his moral nature until it is pure as gold
nurturing his mystic source's jade-like luster
but give him a pull and he won't budge
only when he is willing is he friendly

54   The sunrise in the east the sunset in the west
the bell at dusk the rooster at dawn
the flux of yin and yang has turned my head to snow
over the years I've emptied a hundred crocks of pickles
I plant pines for beams where I find room
I spit out peach pits and make a peach-tree trail
this is for the bow-wary birds in the world
head for the mountains and choose any tree

法道寥寥不可模　一菴深隱是良圖
門前養竹高遮屋　石上分泉直到廚
猊抱子來崖果熟　鶴移巢去礙松枯
禪邊大有閒情緒　收拾乾柴向地爐

浮世光陰有幾何　誰能挈挈又波波
廚空旋去尋黃獨　衲破方思剪綠荷
塵尾罷拈言語斷　佛經忘看蠹魚多
可憐身在袈裟下　趣境攀緣事似麻

55. The spring still flows from the rocks behind Yunlin Temple, the current incarnation of Stonehouse's first hut. But multiple springs also flow behind and in front of his second hut north of the current water-bottling plant. In choosing a location for a hut, hermits always try to build near a water source. Among the fruits I've been surprised to find growing in the mountains in China where hermits dwell are Chinese gooseberries and passion fruit, loquat and dragon eyes.

56. The Chinese yam, or *Dioscorea bulbifera,* is usually collected from the plant's vines in autumn. However, as Stonehouse notes elsewhere, he considered it a food of last resort. Lotus leaves retain their supple yet leathery character through the summer but become dry and brittle as autumn approaches. Hence, they are used as a substitute for cloth only in emergencies or in jest, as here. The whisk is an abbot's symbol of authority and consists of a handle to which the tail of an elk, a deer, or an ox is attached. Stonehouse stopped giving sermons in 1338 after serving as abbot of Fuyuan Temple near Pinghu for seven years.

55   The Way of the Dharma is too singular to copy
     but a well-hidden hut comes close
     I planted bamboo in front to form a screen
     from the rocks I led a spring into my kitchen
     gibbons bring their young to the cliffs when fruits are ripe
     cranes move their nests from the gorge when pines turn brown
     lots of idle thoughts occur during meditation
     I gather the deadwood for my stove

56   There isn't much time in this fleeting life
     why spend it running in circles
     when my kitchen is bare I go look for yams
     when my robe needs a patch I consider lotus leaves
     I've put down the elk tail and stopped giving sermons
     my long-forgotten sutras are home to silverfish
     I pity those who wear a monk's robe
     whose goals and attachments keep them busy

道人緣慮盡　觸目是心光
何處碧桃謝　滿谿流水香
草深蛇性悅　日暖蝶心狂
曾見樵翁說　雲邊雲畫房

一鑊足生涯　居山道者家
有功惟種竹　無暇莫栽花
水碓夜舂米　竹籠春焙茶
人間在何處　隱隱見桑麻

57. The fisherman who discovered the hidden valley in T'ao Yuan-ming's "Peach Blossom Spring" (cf. poem 43) did so by following peach petals upstream to a spring that flowed from a cleft in the rocks.

58. The waterwheels here are pounding rice to remove the husk. Although timber bamboo remains a major product of the hills south of Huchou, Stonehouse was probably more interested in the smaller, edible varieties. Tea leaves are picked several times a year, but those picked in spring are usually the best. Once picked, the leaves are withered in the sun for brief periods then tray-dried in heat-controlled rooms or over a heat source, such as a stove, for shorter or longer periods depending on whether a green, an oolong, or a black/red tea is desired. Mulberry and hemp are usually grown at the margins of farming communities on land unsuitable for rice. Mulberry leaves were used to feed silkworms, which produced the silk that everyone needed to pay their taxes and rent. Hence, most farmers produced silk, but only the very rich actually wore it. Everyone else wore hemp.

57   Followers of the Way are done with reason
wherever they look is the light of the mind
somewhere peach trees are blooming
their petals perfume the stream
deep grass is bliss for a snake
sunshine is butterfly heaven
I heard a woodcutter mention
a lean-to in the clouds

58   A hoe provides a living
for a follower of the Way in the mountains
usually busy planting bamboo
he doesn't have time to grow flowers
a waterwheel hulls his rice at night
a wicker tray dries his tea in spring
where is everyone else
in the haze of hemp and mulberry groves

時時自解顏　年老得安閒
心下渾無事　眼前惟有山
天空鵬翥翼　霧重豹添斑
獨與梅花好　相期盡歲寒

磨煉工夫到　難同知解禪
山空雲自在　天淨月孤圓
盡日閒閒地　長年坦坦然
萬緣休歇罷　一念絕中邊

59. The P'eng is the great bird (at the beginning of *Chuangtzu*) said to be so big it has to climb ninety thousand miles into the sky before it has room to turn. Thus, it is viewed as a symbol of transcendence. In the *Yiching* (49), the leopard that can change its spots is used as a metaphor for the person who succeeds in eliminating vices through the cultivation of virtue. Here, though, it simply disappears by blending with its surroundings. The flowering plum, meanwhile, is a symbol of perseverance in the face of hardship, blossoming during the coldest period of the year.

60. In the seventh line, *mo-lien* (grinding-firing), which I've translated as "yoga or alchemy," refers to the Zen story of grinding a brick to make a mirror — for which see poem 15 and the accompanying note — and also to Taoist alchemical practices aimed at achieving immortality.

59   Most of the time I smile
      old men can take it easy
      not a care in mind
      nothing but mountains before my eyes
      the P'eng soars into the sky
      the leopard blends with the fog
      I'm more like the flowering plum
      waiting for the year-end cold

60   Reasoning comes to an end
      a thought breaks in the middle
      all day nothing but time
      undisturbed all year
      on deserted mountains clouds come and go
      in the clear sky the moon is a lonesome o
      even if yoga or alchemy worked
      it wouldn't match knowing Zen

巖臺舒野望　依約見松門
唐代高僧寺　宋朝丞相墳
溪光晴瀉遠　野色晚來昏
山路歌聲絕　樵歸煙火村

屈曲黃泥路　團團紫槿籬
紙窗開竹屋　瓦竈藝松枝
平澹忘懷處　蕭然絕照時
何人能侶我　無事亦無為

61. Pine Gate is apparently another name for Lone Pine Pass (獨松關), about forty kilometers southwest of Hsiamushan not far from the town of Anchi (安吉). Just inside the pass is Lingfeng Temple (靈峰寺), which dates back to the end of the T'ang. I don't know to which prime minister Stonehouse is referring, but in the vicinity of Lingfeng Temple there are several stupa cemeteries and pagodas dating back to the Sung. The West Fork of the Tiao River also begins just inside the same pass and flows west of Hsiamushan on its way to Taihu Lake. The singing refers to woodcutter work songs. The villages to which Stonehouse is referring were at the foot of the mountain.

62. The hibiscus is found throughout the southern half of China, where it is often grown to form a hedge. Lao-tzu says, "I make no effort / and the people transform themselves / I stay still / and the people correct themselves / I do no work / and the people enrich themselves / I want nothing / and the people simplify themselves" (*Taoteching*: 57).

61   The landscape unrolls from the cliffs
      Pine Gate is there as usual
      a Buddhist temple from the T'ang
      a Sung prime minister's grave
      a river of light drains into the distance
      the wilderness turns dark at dusk
      singing fades from mountain trails
      as woodcutters return to their smoke village

62   A winding muddy trail
      a hedge of purple hibiscus
      a paper-window bamboo hut
      stove-blackened pines
      a simple place where cares disappear
      quiet untroubled days
      who can be like me
      free of work and effort

深山僧住處　端的勝蓬萊
地上並無草　園中却有梅
閒多諸想滅　靜極自心開
一頂破禪衲　和雲曬石臺

一陣從何起　颼颼徧九垓
憾他林木動　吹我竹門開
本自無形段　如何有去來
欲窮窮不到　一虎嘯巖臺

63. Penglai is the abode of Taoist immortals and thought to be located off the north coast of Shantung somewhere in the Pohai Sea. The plum blooms during the coldest time of the year, and throughout Chinese history it has been the friend of recluses looking for any sign of spring.

64. In the last line, all three Ming dynasty editions have "roars," while later editions have "laughs." The Chinese words for "laugh" and "roar" are homophones —both are pronounced *hsiao*. Either way, the tiger is considered the source of wind in China. According to an early Chinese saying recorded in the *Hanshu*, "When a tiger roars, the wind rises. When a dragon stirs, clouds gather" (biography of Wang Pao).

63   A monk's home in the mountains
leaves Penglai in the dust
the ground is free of weeds
there's a plum tree in the garden
fantasies cease there's so much time
the mind opens up it's so quiet
a monk's ragged robe
dries on the rocks next to a cloud

64   Where did that gust come from
whistling across the sky
shaking the trees in the forest
blowing open my bamboo door
without any arms or legs
how does it come and go
my attempts to track it down have failed
from the cliffs a tiger roars

霞霧山頭頂　雲邊闢小房
夏涼窗近竹　冬暖閣朝陽
繭紙衣裳軟　山田粥飯香
此生隨分過　無可得思量

一钁足生涯　長年飽水柴
有山堪寓目　無事可干懷
嵐氣濕茅屋　苔痕上土階
任緣終省力　渾不用安排

65. Hsiawushan is the name that appears on old maps for the mountain's northern summit, which was the location of Stonehouse's second hut. His first hut was near the southern summit labeled Hsiamushan on old maps. People who couldn't afford cloth wore garments made of a heavy grade of paper that included silkworm cocoons unsuitable for silk thread.

66. A thatched covering of grass or rushes is still the most common roofing in the mountains. However, hermits who can afford them use fired clay tiles. If there is one element of Chinese culture most Westerners find incomprehensible, if not exasperating, it's the Chinese glorification of acceptance. But acceptance provides the basis for transcendence, while struggle keeps us enslaved to the dialectic of opposites. At the end of his *Taoteching*, Lao-tzu wrote, "The Way of the Sage / is to act without struggling" (81).

65   From the very top of Hsiawushan
      my hut peers through the clouds
      cool in summer beside bamboo
      warm in winter facing the sun
      cocoon-paper clothes feel soft
      mountain-grown rice smells sweet
      I live on what life brings
      nothing else is worth my time

66   A hoe supplies a living
      there's water and wood all year
      mountains to relax my eyes
      nothing to cause me trouble
      mist soaks through my thatch roof
      moss covers up the steps on the trail
      accepting conserves my strength
      I don't need to arrange a thing

山厨修午供　泉白似銀漿
羹熟筍鞭爛　飯炊粳米香
油煎清頂蕈　醋煮紫芽薑
百味皆難及　何須說上方

真空如湛海　微動即成漚
繚受形骸報　便懷衣食憂
識情奔野馬　妄念走狂猴
不悟空王旨　輪迴卒未休

67. As previously noted, there were springs adjacent to both of Stonehouse's huts. Hard-grain rice refers to a coarse, nonglutinous variety. As for the mushrooms, most likely Stonehouse is referring to *Lactarius indigo,* which is an edible blue mushroom found in forests throughout China. Later editions have the graphically similar *ch'ing-ting* (clear-cap) in place of *ch'ing-ting* (blue-cap), an obvious misprint.

68. At the end of the *Diamond Sutra,* the Buddha says, "As a lamp, a cataract, a star in space / an illusion, a dewdrop, a bubble / a dream, a cloud, a flash of lightning / view all created things like this." And Lao-tzu says, "The reason we have disaster / is because we have a body / if we didn't have a body / we wouldn't have disaster" (*Taoteching:* 13). According to the Buddha, who is referred to here as the Master of Emptiness, the motive forces that move the Wheel of Rebirth are the three poisons of delusion, anger, and desire, chief among which is delusion.

67   Lunch in my mountain kitchen
there's a shimmering springwater sauce
a well-cooked stew of preserved bamboo
a fragrant pot of hard-grain rice
blue-cap mushrooms fried in oil
purple-bud ginger vinaigrette
none of them heavenly dishes
but why should I cater to gods

68   True emptiness is like a translucent sea
where the faintest movement makes foam
as soon as we have a body
we worry about food and clothes
with feelings racing past like horses
and delusions as restless as monkeys
until we understand the Master of Emptiness
the Wheel of Rebirth rolls on

山家八月天　時物自相便
荳莢新垂隴　稻花香滿田
割茅修舊屋　斫竹覓清泉
世上誰知我　優遊樂晚年

茆菴竹樹間　塵世不相關
門對一池水　窗開四面山
煙熏茶竈黑　座蒸布袈斑
不悟空王法　緣何得此間

69. The eighth lunar month in China is roughly equivalent to September. Farmers often take advantage of the hiatus that occurs during this period, when weeding and watering are no longer necessary and harvesting is either over or has not yet begun, to make repairs to their homes and irrigation systems. Where fields are terraced, farmers often grow beans and melons on the banks that separate levels. Bamboo canes are prepared for use as water pipes by dropping hot coals into one end and allowing them to burn through the junctions, or as water conduits by cutting larger bamboos in half lengthwise.

70. Stonehouse's portable tea stove is also mentioned in poem 13. As in poem 68, the Master of Emptiness refers to the Buddha, whose teaching on this subject was often summarized by the lines from the *Heart Sutra:* "Form is emptiness, and emptiness is form."

69   The Eighth Month in the mountains
the seasonal fruits are at hand
new peas hang on terraced banks
rice-flower perfume fills the fields
I cut tall grass to patch my roof
and chop bamboo to channel the spring
who in the world would guess
how carefree and happy I am in old age

70   A thatch hut in a bamboo grove
beyond the world of dust
a pond before the door
mountains out every window
a tea-stove black with soot
a hemp robe streaked with dirt
if I didn't follow the Master of Emptiness
how did I end up here

紅日半銜山　柴門便掩關
綠蒲眠褥軟　白木枕頭彎
松月來先照　溪雲出未還
迢迢清夜夢　不肯到人間

扶杖出松林　閒行上翠岑
鶴群衝鶻散　樹影落溪沉
野果棘難採　藥苗香易尋
澹烟斜日暮　紅葉半巖陰

71. In poem 27, the mountain bites the sun. Here, the sun bites the mountain. In both cases, as in Hui-neng's response to the argument in the *Platform Sutra* about a flag moving in the wind, it's the mind that does the biting. Until fairly recently, the Chinese preferred to sleep on hard pillows designed to cool the brain. In addition to making pillows of wood, they also used porcelain.

72. When Buddhist monks or nuns venture into the mountains, they often carry a six-foot staff with rings on the top that jangle, announcing their presence to wild animals, and with a small spade at the bottom for negotiating slippery slopes or for digging up the odd root.

71   As soon as the red sun bites the mountain
I shut my rickety door
I sleep on a mattress of soft green grass
and the curve of a wooden pillow
and when the moon shines through the pines
before clouds return to the stream
clear night dreams go far
but not to the world of men

72   I hiked staff in hand beyond the pines
and found myself on an emerald peak
a flock of cranes were chasing a hawk
tree shadows darkened the streams
thorns made wild fruit hard to pick
their scent made herbs easy to find
thin smoke veiled the sinking sun
red leaves shaded half the cliff

好山千萬疊　屋占最高層
減塑三尊佛　長明一椀燈
鐘敲寒夜月　茶煮石池冰
客問西來意　惟言我不能

取捨與行藏　人生各有方
乾坤容我懶　名利使他忙
背日鷗眠埠　營巢燕遠梁
情迷隨物轉　不得悟空王

73. The Buddhist trinity is usually represented by Amita, Shakyamuni, and Maitreya, the buddhas of the past, the present, and the future. A small handbell is often used while chanting. At the end of the fifth century, Bodhidharma left his home in South India and brought the teaching of Zen to China. Originally, the word *dhyana* (which the Chinese at that time pronounced *zen-na*) meant "meditation." Following Bodhidharma's arrival, the word was also used to refer to his technique of pointing directly to the mind, and it was eventually applied to the lineage of teachers and disciples who followed this teaching. A favorite *kung-an* (or koan in Japanese) was, "Why did Bodhidharma come from the West?" — "the West" in this case referred to India.

74. In the *Analects,* Confucius advises his disciples, "Come forward when you are of use. Retire when you are not" (7.10). Heaven and Earth represent the basic dialectic of yin and yang. The Master of Emptiness refers to the Buddha, who taught that since all things depend on other things for their existence, they are themselves empty of self-existence, and thus not ultimately real.

73   On a ten-thousand-story-high mountain
      my hut sits at the very top
      I shaped three buddhas from clay
      and keep an oil lamp burning
      I ring a bell cold moonlit nights
      and brew tea with pond ice
      but when someone asks what coming from the West means
      I can't say a word

74   Advancing or retiring grasping or letting go
      people all have their own ways
      Heaven and Earth let me be lazy
      profit and fame put others to work
      gulls sleep on piers with their backs to the sun
      swallows build nests above house beams
      misled by passion distracted by things
      they remain unaware of the Master of Emptiness

結草便為菴　年年用覆苫
紙窗松葉暗　竹屋蘚花粘
麥飯惟饒火　藜羹不點塩
生涯隨分過　誰管世人嫌

75. The paper used for windows was treated with oil to make it waterproof. Although mosses are nonflowering plants, their spore capsules are sometimes borne on long stems that suggest those of a flower. Wheat gruel is made by grinding wheat together with its husk and boiling the resulting mixture with wild or cultivated vegetables. Pigweed soup is also mentioned in poem 45. Wheat gruel and pigweed soup were once among the survival foods of the poor. Lao-tzu says, "The best are like water / bringing help to all / without competing / choosing what others avoid / they thus approach the Tao" (*Taoteching*: 8).

75   I weave rush grass for my hut
every year a new layer of thatch
pine trees shade the paper windows
moss flowers decorate the bamboo walls
for wheat gruel I only need fire
and pigweed soup requires no salt
I survive on whatever comes my way
why should I mind what others hate

妻妻茅舍新秋夜
山月如銀牽老興
白荳花開絡緯啼
閒行不覺過峰西

滿山筍蕨滿園茶
大抵四時春最好
一樹紅花間白花
就中猶好是山家

76. A poem written on the Mid-Autumn Festival, when the Chinese celebrate the harvest. Next to the Lunar New Year, this is the most important annual celebration in China, and family members make every effort to be together this night, which occurs on the full moon of the eighth lunar month, usually in September. I'm guessing the flowers in this case are those of the hyacinth bean (*Dolichos lablab*), which blooms throughout the summer and autumn in this part of the Yangtze watershed.

77. Fiddleheads have been standard hermit fare in China ever since Shu-ch'i and his brother, Po-yi, tried to survive on a diet of little else ca. 1100 BC. Spring is also the best time to pick the leaves of most varieties of tea. In its natural state, the tea tree can grow as tall as any other tree, but it is usually kept pruned waist-high to make picking its leaves easier. Hsiamushan teas include white, green, and red varieties, and are famous in the Huchou area. The second line suggests a peach tree in a group of plum trees. Normally, the plum blooms before the peach, but in poem 40, Stonehouse reports both flowering together on Hsiamushan.

SEVEN-SYLLABLE QUATRAINS

76   A thatch hut is lonely on a new fall night
with white peas in flower and crickets calling
mountain-moon silver evokes an old joy
suddenly I've strolled west of the peak

77   Mountains of fiddleheads garden of tea
one tree of pink mixed in with the white
of all the seasons spring is the best
a mountain home then is especially fine

有人問我何年住　坐久纔方省得來
門外碧桃親手種　春光二十度花開

厭煩勞役愛安閒　箇樣如何居得山
百丈已前巖穴士　生涯全在钁頭邊

78. Stonehouse must have planted this tree as soon as he arrived at Hsiamu-shan, which, according to poem 170, was in 1312. Because he left to become abbot of Fuyuan Monastery near Pinghu in May 1331, this poem would have been written shortly before his departure.

79. Pai-chang (百丈, 720–814) is credited with establishing the basic rules still used in Zen monasteries, which have often been summarized as "No work, no food." Paichang was the name of the mountain he lived on. The mountain is one hundred kilometers west of Nanchang, the capital of Kiangsi, and it was by the mountain's name that he was better known, rather than by his monastic name, Huai-hai (懷海).

78   Someone asked what year I arrived
     I had to think before the answer came
     the peach tree I planted outside my door
     has flowered in spring twenty times

79   If you hate hard work and like to loaf
     how will you survive in the mountains
     Pai-chang made his home among cliffs and caves
     and his living depended completely on his hoe

年老菴居養病身
怕寒起坐燒松火
日高猶自未開門
一曲樵歌隔塢聞

童子未曾歸動火
山菴喜免征徭慮
水雲早已到投齋
賸種青松只賣柴

80. This would have been written after Stonehouse retired as abbot of Fuyuan Temple and moved to the mountain's northern summit, or Hsiawushan. The cold has forced him to consider a fire of something more than the usual leaves and twigs. In China, woodcutters sing to accompany the rhythm of their work. Stonehouse may also be alluding to the hermit-poet Chu Tun-ju (朱敦儒, 1081–1159), who titled one of his collections *Woodcutter Songs*. Chu retired to Chia-hsing, a prefecture not far from where Stonehouse served as abbot.

81. Before a man or woman can be ordained as a Buddhist monk or nun, they must first spend several years as a novice under the guidance of a senior monk or nun. Here, novices visit Stonehouse seeking instruction. But while they might arrive in the morning to pay their respects, they are gone by nightfall. Once ordained, monks and nuns are allowed to wander at will and stay at any temple where they can find room. But they, too, prefer life in a monastery to life in a mountain hut. During the Yuan dynasty, monks were exempt from corvée, or forced labor on state projects. In addition to firewood, hermits sell or barter wild herbs, nuts, and fruits to obtain such necessities as salt, rice or wheat flour, cooking oil, lamp oil, and cloth.

80   Old and retired I nurse a sick body
       long after sunrise my door is still closed
       shivering I get up to start a pine fire
       from the next valley over I hear a woodcutter's song

81   Novices don't stay to stir the fire
       wandering monks prefer free meals
       hermits at least avoid corvée and taxes
       and plant enough pines to live off firewood

玉堂銀燭笙歌夜　金谷羅幃富貴家
爭似道人茅屋下　一天晴月曬梅花

相逢盡說世途難　自向菴中討不安
除却淵明賦歸去　更無一箇肯休官

82. The appellation *jade hall* was first applied to the imperial palace and in particular to the women's apartments. By Stonehouse's day, however, the term was usually reserved for the Hanlin Academy, which housed the country's most prestigious scholars. Shih Ch'ung (石崇, 249–300) held ostentatious banquets at a place called Gold Valley in the Peimang Hills north of Loyang. Whenever a guest failed to drain his cup, Shih had one of the serving girls beheaded, or so one story went.

83. T'ao Yuan-ming lived in the late fourth and early fifth centuries and is revered as one of China's greatest poets, certainly its greatest poet extolling the retired life. Finding the demands of government service not to his liking, he quit his post and retired to a farmstead at the foot of Lushan (廬山) at the age of forty. T'ao celebrated his decision in his "Ode to Retirement," which began "Oh, let me retire / let socializing end and wandering stop / let the world and me say goodbye."

82   Jade-hall silver-candle nights of song
      gold-valley silk-curtain homes of the rich
      can't compare with a hermit's thatch hut
      where plum blossoms bask in unclouded moonlight

83   All those I meet say the world's ways are hard
      even in a hut they can't find peace
      besides Yuan-ming announcing his retirement
      who else mentions resigning

山厨寂寂斷炊煙
面壁老僧無定力
凍鎖泉聲欲雪天
又思乞食到人間

種了冬瓜便種茄
眾人若要厨堂好
勞形苦骨做生涯
須是園頭常在家

84. The most distinctive sound of a traditional kitchen in ancient, and even not so ancient, China was that of the bellows, which was built into the side of the stove with a handle that could be pumped whenever more air was needed. There was a spring near each of Stonehouse's two huts on the mountain. The practice of "wall contemplation" was associated with Bodhidharma, who was said to have spent nine years sitting in a cave near Shaolin Temple meditating upon the cave's rock wall before he transmitted his understanding to Hui-k'o (慧可), who then became Zen's Second Patriarch. According to his contemporaries, Stonehouse preferred surviving on wild plants to begging.

85. In the Yangtze watershed, winter melon, or *Benincasa cerifera,* and Chinese eggplant, or *Solanum melongena,* both bear their fruit well into autumn. Neither requires much effort to grow, and both are easily preserved, the former with heat and vinegar, the latter with stove ashes.

84   There's nothing going on in my mountain kitchen
      I hear the spring melting but the sky says snow
      facing the wall meditating in vain
      again this old monk thinks of begging in town

85   I plant winter melon then aubergine
      I wear myself out staying alive
      but someone who wants a decent kitchen
      needs to keep a garden nearby

粥去飯來何日了　日生月落幾時休
都來與我無干涉　空起許多閒念頭

屋後青松八九樹　門前紫芋兩三鱗
山居道者機關少　家火從頭說向人

86. Because it's easier to digest, rice porridge is usually eaten in the morning, while steamed rice is the standard staple at lunch and dinner. The only difference is the amount of water used in cooking.

87. Taro, or *Colocasia esculenta*, is one of the principal starches of hermits in the southern half of China. In the last line, the term *chia-huo* (home-fire) nowadays means "tools," but in the past it also meant "provisions" or "means of support," which is how Stonehouse uses the same term in poem 154 as well.

86   Will the porridge or rice ever end
will the sun or moon ever rest
either way it's no concern of mine
so many fantasies arise in vain

87   Eight or nine pines behind his hut
two or three mounds of taro in front
a mountain recluse doesn't have many interests
all he talks about are his provisions

此事誰人敢強為　除非知有莫能知
分明月在梅花上　看到梅花早已遲

過了事已過去了　未來不必預思量
只今便道只今句　梅子熟時梔子香

88. Zen Buddhists liken any teaching to a finger pointing to the moon: once
you've seen the moon, you don't need to look at the finger.

89. In the lower Yangtze watershed, plums ripen and gardenias bloom in the
fifth lunar month.

88   This is something no one can force
       besides knowing it's there there's nothing to know
       once the moon shines above a flowering plum
       it's too late to look at the blossoms

89   What's gone is already gone
       and what hasn't come needs no thought
       right now I'm writing a right-now line
       plums are ripe and gardenias in bloom

一日打眠三五度　也消不得許多閒

循環數徧琅玕竹　又出青松望遠山

攀緣起倒易消停　卒急難除是愛憎

我笑青山高突兀　青山嫌我瘦稜層

90. The kind of jade mentioned as hyperbole here is an iridescent variety found in the Kunlun Mountains of myth where plants are made of precious stones.

91. Love (desire), hate (anger), and delusion make up the three poisons that turn the Wheel of Rebirth.

90   Three or four naps every day
     still don't exhaust all my free time
     I walk around the jade bamboo a few times
     then hike past the pines and gaze at far mountains

91   The flux of attachments is easy to stop
     but it's hard all at once to end love and hate
     I laugh at the mountain for towering so high
     and the mountain mocks me for being so skinny

真空湛寂惟常在　不覺良由妄所朦
真性何曾離妄有　花開花落自春風

天湖水湛琉璃碧　霞霧山圍錦幛紅
觸目本來成現事　何須叉手問禪翁

92. True emptiness is also empty of emptiness and thus includes all things.

93. Sky Lake was the name Stonehouse gave to the pond formed by the spring near his first hut on the mountain's southern summit. According to the sutras of Pure Land Buddhism, the ground of Amita's Western Paradise is made of aquamarine, which ranks first among the gemstones that are Buddhism's seven jewels. Hsiawu, or Redfog, was the name for the mountain's northern summit and where Stonehouse built his second hut and dug a second pond he also called Sky Lake. Silk brocade remains among the most famous products of the nearby Hangchou area.

92   True emptiness is clear and always present
masked by delusions for reasons we don't know
how could what is real and false exist apart
flowers bloom and flowers fall when the spring wind blows

93   Sky Lake is a pool of aquamarine
Redfog is a screen of crimson brocade
regarding what is present before your eyes
why press your hands together and ask an old monk

年老氣衰真箇懶　晨朝更不見和南

客來無語相衹對　辛苦空勞到草菴

老去一身都是懶　閒來百念盡成灰

與兄相見畧彈指　無奈人情強接陪

94. Among the Buddhist and Taoist hermits I've encountered in China, they all conduct some sort of ceremony at dawn and again at night involving chanting and meditation.

94   Old and exhausted I'm truly lazy
        no folded hands at dawn anymore
        to those who visit I have nothing to say
        their trek to my hut is such a waste of effort

95   Old through and through I'm utterly lazy
        a hundred fantasies all turn to ash
        but the moment a friend arrives
        inescapable feelings force me up

田地無塵長不掃　柴門有客扣方開
雪晴斜月侵簷冷　梅影一枝窗上來

茅屋低低三兩間　團團環遶盡青山
竹牀不許閒雲宿　日未斜時便掩關

96. It is customary when expecting guests to sweep the path in front of one's house and to leave the door ajar. Here, Stonehouse receives visitors that require no such preparation.

97. The Chinese measurement known as a *chien* was used for taxation and sumptuary purposes. It was the distance between two pillars or posts that supported the roof beams (or *chia*) of a building. Its actual length varied anywhere from three to four feet, or about the width of a mat. Elsewhere, Stonehouse talks about his "wooden bed." I imagine he tried several kinds in the course of thirty-four years. The "cloud" also conjures the image of a visiting monk. For another version of this poem see poem 129.

96   There's no dust to sweep on a mountain
        guests have to knock before I open the door
        after a snowfall the setting moon slips through the eaves
        a plum branch shadow comes right to the window

97   My hut is two maybe three mats wide
        surrounded by mountains on every side
        my cot couldn't fit a cloud for the night
        I shut the door before sunset

禪兄何事到煙蘿　老我生涯苦不多
巖下木樨香滿樹　園中菜甲綠成窠

一片無塵新雨地　半邊有蘚古時松
目前景物人皆見　取用誰知各不同

98. The smoke was that of the sticks of incense used to measure time in the meditation hall, and the "vines" were the tangled logic of the koans used for instruction at Zen monasteries.

99. Lao-tzu wrote, "Existence makes a thing useful / but nonexistence makes it work" (*Taoteching*: 11). Pointing to a huge, gnarled oak tree, Chuang-tzu (莊子) said, "It's because its wood is useless that it has lived to such great age" (*Chuangtzu*: 4.6).

98   Why do my Zen friends choose smoke and vines
     this life of mine isn't so hard
     gardenias below the cliff perfume the trees
     shoots in my garden form rows of green

99   A clean patch of ground after a rain
     an ancient pine half-covered with moss
     such things appear before our eyes
     but what we do with them isn't the same

萬境萬機俱寢息　一知一見盡消融
閒閒兩耳全無用　坐到晨鷄與暮鐘

巖房終日寂寥寥　世念何曾有一毫
雖著衣裳喫粥飯　恰如死了未曾燒

100. The bell was probably that of Fuyuan Temple at the northeast foot of the mountain near the present village of Yangshuwu (楊樹塢). However, during Stonehouse's second stay on the mountain, he was joined by other monks, and perhaps by that time there was a hermitage big enough to require something other than a handbell.

101. Although burial has always been common in China, during the Yuan dynasty cremation became popular. However, it became so popular and wood sufficiently scarce that the government was compelled to issue a decree forbidding the practice, except for monks and nuns.

100   Ten thousand schemes and fantasies have ended
       all that I've known and seen has vanished
       my two fine ears are no good at all
       I sit past the cockcrow and the evening bell

101   My home in the cliffs is like a tomb
       barren of even one worldly thought
       although I eat food and wear clothes
       it's as if I were dead but not yet cremated

門前枯木似人立　屋後好山如浪堆

老我為人無可說　高高雲路賺兄來

山形凹凸路高低　石占雲頭屋占蹊

地窄栽來蔬菜少　又營小圃在橋西

103. In addition to the current road built in the 1950s during the construction of a radar station on the summit, there are four trails, all of them lined at various points with stone slabs. Normally, such trails are not made by farmers or herb collectors but by pilgrims, and they probably didn't exist in that form during Stonehouse's day, as it was Stonehouse who first "opened up" the mountain. The second line is intended as a pun on Stonehouse's name. Most likely, the stream here is the one that forms at the northern summit and flows down the mountain's north slope alongside the trail that leads to the village of Yangshuwu. There is, in fact, an ancient bridge between the foot of the mountain and the village.

102   There's a snag in front like a standing man
a ridge in back like a curling wave
as for me there's nothing to say
it's the road through the clouds that lures people here

103   Up-and-down mountain zigzag trail
stone in the clouds house by a stream
land too scarce to grow much
I even farm west of the bridge

百年日月閒中度　八萬塵勞靜處消
綠水光中山影轉　紅爐焰上雪花飄
西方有路不肯去　地獄無門闖要過
金閣銀臺仙子少　鑊湯爐炭罪人多

104. Some Buddhist pundit once counted the number of afflictions to this mortal coil and came up with eighty-four thousand.

105. The Western Paradise of Amita Buddha features platforms and pavilions and even trees made of the seven jewels: gold, silver, aquamarine, crystal, coral, carnelian, and nacre (the iridescent lining of the giant clam). Buddhists count eighteen cold hells and eighteen hot ones.

104 A hundred years slip by unnoticed
    eighty-four thousand cares dissolve in stillness
    a mountain image shimmers on sunlit water
    snowflakes swirl above a glowing stove

105 There's a road to the West nobody takes
    people struggle to a escape a hell with no gate
    jeweled towers and pavilions see few immortals
    cauldrons and ovens welcome the wicked

著意求真真轉遠　擬心斷妄妄猶多
道人一種平懷處　月在青天影在波

要求作佛真箇易　唯斷妄心真箇難
幾度霜天明月夜　坐來覺得五更寒

107. Yung-chia's *Song of Enlightenment* begins: "Does no one else see / the idle follower of the Way / neither working nor studying / neither ending delusions nor seeking the truth?"

106   Try to find what's real and what's real becomes more distant
try to end delusions and delusions multiply
followers of the Way have an all-embracing place
the moon in the sky and its reflection in the waves

107   Trying to become a buddha is easy
but ending delusions is hard
how many frosty moonlit nights
have I sat until I felt the cold before dawn

萬緣脫去心無事　諸有空來性坦然
幾度夜窓虛吐白　月和流水到門前

一事無心萬事休　也無歡喜也無憂
無心莫謂便無事　尚有無心箇念頭

108. Buddhists recognize twenty-five kinds of existence: fourteen in the realm of desire, seven in the realm of form, and four in the formless realm. Stonehouse channeled the spring flowing from the rocks behind his hut into a pond that he dug in his yard.

109. Here, "no-mind" refers to the fourth and highest state of meditation in the realm of form, which is devoid of all thought but still subject to karma and thus impermanence.

108   Stripped of conditions my mind is at rest
emptied of existence my nature is at peace
how often at night have my windows turned white
as the moon and stream passed by my door

109   Work with no mind and all work stops
no more joy and no more sorrow
but don't think no mind means you're done
there is still the thought of no-mind

於事無心風過樹　於心無事月行空
風聲月色消磨盡　去却一重還一重

新年頭了舊年尾　明日四兮今日三
道業未成空白首　大千無處著羞慚

110. Our false mind is an illusion, and our true mind cannot be grasped. Hence, Buddhists sometimes call our true mind "no mind." The expression "No mind in work, no work in mind" was a saying attributed to the ninth-century Zen master Te-shan (德山).

111. The second line refers to the third and fourth days of the year, when the new moon first becomes visible. The Chinese calculate their ages not from their birthdays, but from New Year's Day. Hence, the holiday often reminds people of the ephemeral nature of life.

110 No mind in my work the wind blows through the trees
no work in my mind the moon crosses the sky
windsound and moonlight wear away
one layer then another

111 New year head old year tail
tomorrow the fourth today the third
the Way unattained I have grown old in vain
where in the world can I express my shame

白髮催人瘦入肩
裩無腰帶袴無口
住來茅屋已多年
一領偏衫沒半邊

青山不着臭屍骸
顧我也無三昧火
死了何須掘土埋
光前絕後一堆柴

112. In the last line, Stonehouse is referring to the kasaya, which monks wear like a toga over one shoulder. It thus covers only half as much of the upper body as a regular robe. Although it is standard attire among Buddhists in Sri Lanka and Southeast Asia, in China it is usually reserved for begging and for temple ceremonies.

113. All hermits have a favorite text they read or chant every day, but I have never seen a copy of the *Lankavatara* in a hut. Nowadays, it's usually the *Lotus* or *Titsang* sutras. But then, times have changed. I'm guessing Stonehouse is referring to the course followed by the stream near his first hut, which flowed down the east slope of Hsiamushan toward Shaokang Village.

112   Head of white hair shoulders all bones
I've lived in a hut more years than I can count
my shorts have no drawstring my pants have no legs
and half of my robe is missing

113   Before I can finish the *Lankavatara*
sunset shadows flow east with the stream
clouds return and I retire to my hut
a day of light and shade ends early again

一軸楞伽看未周　夕陽斜影水東流
雲歸自就茅簷宿　一日光陰又早休

茅簷雨過日頭紅　瞬息陰晴便不同
況是死生呼吸事　黃昏難保聽朝鐘

114. This poem, which Stonehouse wrote down just before he died, appears between poems 113 and 115 in all three Ming dynasty copies but does not appear in later editions. I'm guessing it was simply the poem that came to mind as he was asked for a few parting words when he was dying. I'm also guessing later editors deleted it because it was his death poem, and they reasoned it wouldn't have been part of the *Mountain Poems,* which Stonehouse finished before he died. The term *samadhi* refers to deep meditation where the separation between subject and object disappears. The "family line" is the karma one accumulates that leads to further rebirth and suffering.

114   Corpses don't stink in the mountains
there's no need to bury them deep
I might not have the fire of samadhi
but enough wood to end this family line

115   Rain soaks my hut then the sun shines
weather can change in the blink of an eye
but not as fast as the breath of existence
at dusk it's hard to hear the morning bell

明明見了非他見　了了常知無別知

記得去秋煙雨裏　猿來偷去一雙梨

半窓松影半窓月　一箇蒲團一箇僧

盤膝坐來中夜後　飛蛾撲滅佛前燈

116   No one else sees what I see clearly
       no one else knows what I know well
       I recall one misty day last fall
       a gibbon came here and stole two pears

117   Half the window pine shadows half the window moon
       a solitary cushion a solitary monk
       sitting cross-legged after midnight
       when a moth puts out the altar lamp

長年心裏渾無事　每日菴中樂有餘

飯罷濃煎茶喫了　池邊坐石數游魚

飯炊五合黃陳米　羹煮數莖青薺苗

淡薄自然滋味好　何須更要着薑椒

118. The ability of tea to allay hunger and to quench thirst as well as to clear the senses without overstimulating them has made it the drink of choice among those who meditate.

119. The expression *ch'en-huang-mi* (old rice) refers to rice left over from the last harvest, and *wu-k'o* (a quarter pint or "bowl"), which is still used in Chinese pharmacies for 100ml, suggests Stonehouse was rationing it out until the new harvest was in. Shepherd's purse (*Capsella bursa-pastoris*) was associated with hardship simply because it grew wild. But it was, and still is, the vegetable of choice in such prepared foods as dumplings.

118   Not one care in mind all year
        I find enough joy every day in my hut
        and after a meal and a pot of strong tea
        I sit on a rock by the pond and count fish

119   For dinner I cook a bowl of old rice
        and a soup of shepherd's purse greens
        bland but natural flavors are fine
        who needs to add ginger or spice

移家深入亂峰西　煙樹重重隔遠溪
年老心閒貪睡穩　厭聞鐘響與鷄啼

山風吹破故窓紙　片片雪花飛入來
添盡布裘渾不煖　拾枯深撥地爐灰

120. In the first of his *Mountain Poems,* Stonehouse says he moved west of Huchou (Cha River). Between Huchou and Hsiamushan there are a dozen smaller mountains, but the actual direction was more southerly than westerly. The distance, meanwhile, was less than twenty-five kilometers. The second line most likely refers to the East Fork of the Tiao River.

121. Stonehouse often mentions his clay tea stove and sometimes refers to the stove he used for cooking, but here he refers to what would have been a brick- or stone-lined small pit in the middle of the earthen floor of his hut.

120   I moved west into a maze of peaks
        put trees and mist between me and the distant river
        old and untroubled I like to sleep late
        I hate to hear roosters or bells

121   Mountain wind ripped out my old paper windows
        snowflakes swirl inside
        my once-padded robe isn't warm anymore
        I probe the hearth with a stick

半窗斜日冷生光　破衲蒙頭坐竹床
枯葉滿爐燒焰火　不知屋上有寒霜

幾樹山花紅灼灼　一池春水綠漪漪
衲僧若具超宗眼　不待無情為發機

122. Stonehouse is being facetious. Burning leaves in the stove as winter night approaches suggests he is out of firewood.

123. Ah, the peach trees.

122   The setting sun's cold light fills half the window
        sitting on my bamboo bed with my ragged robe across my head
        and the stove ablaze with dry leaves
        I would never guess there's frost on the roof

123   A few trees in bloom radiant red
        a pond in spring rippling green
        a monk with eyes that see beyond Zen
        doesn't have to be dead to use them

雲未歸時便掩扃
山家不養鷄和犬
柴牀眠穩思冥冥
日到茅簷夢未醒

粥去飯來茶喫了
細推百億閻浮界
開窓獨坐看青山
白日無人似我閒

125. Rice is watered-down for breakfast and steamed or boiled at other meals. Tea is drunk as an aid to digestion and to dispel fatigue. Stonehouse also tells us he drank his tea strong. Jambu is the short form of Jambudvipa. According to ancient Indian geography, the world was divided into four continents, with Jambudvipa constituting all of Asia.

124   I shut my door before the clouds return
       on my cot I sleep deep my thoughts unseen
       hermits don't raise dogs or chickens
       the sun warms my roof and I still dream

125   After porridge after rice after drinking tea
       I open the window and sit and gaze at mountains
       survey every realm throughout Jambu
       during the day no one is more idle than me

黑霧濃雲撥不開　忽然去了忽然來
任他伎倆自磨滅　紅日依前照石臺

一天紅日曉東南　自拔青苗插瘦田
布襏半沾泥水濕　歸來脫曬竹房前

126. "To push away the clouds in order to see the sun" was an old saying the Chinese used when someone was trying to remove insurmountable obstructions from their path.

127. As the days of autumn and winter become shorter and darker, the place where the sun rises moves progressively southward. Hence, its reappearance on the southeastern horizon marks the advent of spring.

126   Dense fog and clouds too thick to push away
suddenly appear and suddenly depart
clever people can wear themselves out
the sun lights the rocks the same as before

127   As soon as the sun lights the southeast sky
I transplant sprouts into rocky fields
my robe half-soaked with mud
I take off and dry in front of my hut

喫桃吐核核成樹　樹大花開又結桃
春去秋來知幾度　爭教我不白頭毛

茅屋方方一丈慳　四簷松竹四圍山
老僧自住尚狹窄　那許雲來借半間

128. The peach is native to China and appears in the archaeological record of the Hangchou area as early as five thousand years ago. In poem 78, Stonehouse dates his arrival on Hsiamushan by the peach tree he planted outside his door.

129. The expression *chang-fang* (ten-foot square) originally referred to an abbot's room and was later used to refer to the abbot himself. In the last line, the cloud could also refer to a monk or nun on pilgrimage.

128   I eat a peach spit out the pit the pit becomes a tree
the tree grows and flowers and makes another peach
spring departs and fall arrives year after year
how can I keep my hair from turning white

129   My hut isn't quite ten feet across
surrounded by pines bamboo and mountains
an old monk hardly has room for himself
much less for a visiting cloud

臨機切莫避刀鎗　拚死和他戰一塲
打得趙州關子破　大千無處不皈降

有限光陰一百年　幾人得到百年全
縱饒百歲終歸死　只是相分後與前

130. Chao-chou (趙州) and his teacher Nan-ch'uan (南泉) were among the most renowned Zen masters of the ninth century. One day when Chao-chou was working alone in the monastery kitchen, he shut the door and let the room fill with smoke then cried, "Fire!" When the other monks came running, he said, "Say the right word, and I'll open the door!" But none of the monks could think of anything to say. Finally, when Nan-ch'uan arrived, he handed Chao-chou a lock through the window, and Chao-chou opened the door (*Chuantenglu*: 10). According to Buddhists, a universe consists of a billion worlds (one thousand to the power of three).

130   Don't run away when he strikes
        make it a fight to the death
        break down Chao-chou's door
        the whole universe will surrender

131   Our time is confined to one hundred years
        but which of us gets them all
        hundred-year-olds die too
        the only difference is sooner or later

溪邊黃葉水去住　嶺上白雲風往來
爭似老僧常不動　長年無事坐巖臺

一大藏經閒故紙　一千七百葛藤窠
誰能去討他分曉　起箇念頭猶是多

132. Among the works listed in the Buddhist Canon, or Tripitaka, is a series of five Sung dynasty works (the *Chuantenglu* and its companion volumes) that include some seventeen hundred koans. Elsewhere, Stonehouse uses the word *vines* in reference to koans. Note, too, that the Chinese used vines in the production of paper.

132   The whole Buddhist Canon is worthless old paper
       seventeen hundred tangled vines
       who can see through the mess
       one thought is still too many

133   Leaves along the shore stop and flow with the stream
       clouds above the ridge come and go with the wind
       no match for an old monk who doesn't move
       who does nothing but sit among the cliffs all year

霞霧山高路又遙
却嫌住處太危險

菴居從簡篾三條
落賺多人登陟勞

老覺形枯氣力衰
自憐不解藏踪跡

客來勉強出衹陪
松食荷衣憶大梅

134. Again, Stonehouse uses Hsiawu (Redfog) as the name of the mountain's northern summit, where he was living when he wrote this poem—as opposed to Hsiamu, the name of the southern summit, where he first lived.

135. Pine meal, which can include pine nuts and pine pollen, has kept many recluses from starving and provided a rare treat for others. Lotus-leaf attire is not entirely imaginary, though it is usually associated with immortals, as in a poem by Ch'u Yuan (d. 278 BC) entitled "The Lesser Lord of Long Life": "A lotus-leaf robe and a belt of vines / suddenly he appears and suddenly departs." Ta-mei, or Big Plum, was a disciple of Ma-tsu. Following his enlightenment, he moved so far into the mountains people thought he had died. Then one day, a monk who had lost his way stumbled into a clearing and discovered Big Plum sitting in front of a hut. Not long afterward, Ta-mei had so many disciples he wished he had moved deeper into the mountains (*Chuantenglu*: 7).

134   Hsiawu is high and the trail is long
       and my hut is nothing but bamboo and vines
       despite their dislike of dangerous places
       people are still fooled into making the climb

135   I feel old and decrepit and weaker by the day
       but visitors force me up
       I regret not learning to cover my tracks
       but lotus clothes and pine cakes call Big Plum to mind

道人屋冷四簷竹　長者門高百尺墻
屋冷道人心愈靜　門高長者日多忙

盡道凡心非佛性　我言佛性即凡心
工夫只怕無人做　鐵杵磨教作線針

136. Repressed by the Confucian values of earlier governments, merchants were given unprecedented freedom and power during the Yuan dynasty, when the Mongols made extensive use of their services in collecting taxes and financing state projects.

137. Buddhists agree that we all possess the potential to become buddhas but differ as to how the realization of buddhahood takes place. While most sects say it is realized in stages and through moral discipline and meditation, the Zen sect prefers the radical approach of Bodhidharma: "If you could find your buddha nature apart from your mortal nature, where would it be? Our mortal nature is our buddha nature. Beyond this nature, there is no buddha" (*The Zen Teaching of Bodhidharma*: pp. 16–17). Thus, Zen masters point to the everyday mind.

136   A hermit's hut is lonely encircled by bamboo
        a merchant's gate is high with hundred-foot-long walls
        in his lonely hut a hermit finds peace
        behind his high gate a merchant finds none

137   People say everyday mind isn't our buddha nature
        I say our buddha nature is simply everyday mind
        afraid no one will do any work
        they teach grinding iron rods to make needles

南北東西去復還　陸行車馬水行船

利名門路如天遠　走殺世間人萬千

居山那得有工夫　種了冬瓜便種瓠

設使一毫功不及　許多田地盡荒蕪

138. Long before the Grand Canal was completed, an extensive system of small canals and natural waterways enabled people to do much of their long-distance traveling in China by boat. The system of roads was even more extensive and was maintained by the government to ensure its continued control over the territory it administered.

139. For winter melons, see my note to poem 85. Gourds, or *Lagenaria vulgaris,* were grown for use as containers and utensils as well as for food.

138   East or west north or south then back again
      by cart or horse on land by boat on water
      the gate to fame and fortune is as far away as Heaven
      yet people by the million kill themselves to reach it

139   What sort of work takes place in the mountains
      planting winter melons then planting gourds
      and if your efforts fall a bit short
      most of your fields end up beneath weeds

離眾多年無坐具　入山長久沒袈裟
單單有箇鐵鐺子　留待人來煮瀑花

布衣破綻種青麻　粮食無時刈早禾
辛苦做來牽補過　復身免得報檀那

140. A meditation cushion and a robe for wearing in public were part of every Zen monk's or nun's gear. This particular kind of pot was made of iron or clay and had three feet, which enabled it to be placed over a charcoal fire. Stonehouse would have used it for boiling water for tea, others for heating wine.

141. According to his contemporaries, Stonehouse refused to beg for food.

140 Too long away from monasteries I don't have a cushion
   too long in the mountains I don't have a robe
   all I have is an iron pot
   to entertain guests with bubbling water

141 When my clothes come apart I plant hemp
   when my food runs out I harvest rice early
   I pull myself through with effort
   and when I'm better I don't owe any alms

山居活計钁頭邊　衣食須營豈自然
種稻下田泥沒膝　賣柴出市擔磨肩

我已盡形無別念　任他作佛與生天
飯香麥麨和松粉　採好藤花雜筍鞭

142. Pine pollen is collected in late spring or early summer. "Vine flowers" refers to wisteria blossoms, which are removed individually from each raceme and stir-fried. At the monastery in Taiwan where I lived for several years, we dined throughout the summer on stir-fried daylily blossoms, picked a day or two before they were due to open. Among the mountain-dwelling Aini in Yunnan province, I also enjoyed stir-fried bauhinia flowers.

143. Hermits usually need to sell or trade something to get the few things they can't grow or gather on the mountains where they live. If it isn't firewood, it's herbs or other mountain products. One Buddhist nun I met in the Chungnan Mountains south of Sian was able to buy everything she needed with the harvest from four walnut trees.

142   Parched wheat and pine pollen make a fine meal
       vine flowers and salted bamboo make a tasty dish
       when I'm exhausted I think of nothing else
       let others become buddhas or immortals

143   Life in the mountains depends on a hoe
       food and clothes don't appear by themselves
       I'm knee-deep in mud planting rice in a field
       or my shoulders are sore from hauling firewood to town

鑺頭添鐵屋頭懸　健即鋤雲倦即眠
紅日正中黃獨熟　甘香不在火爐邊

團團一箇尖頭屋　外面誰知裏面寬
世界大千都着了　尚餘閒地放蒲團

144. The Chinese yam, unlike its cousins in the sweet potato family, is not especially meaty or sweet and needs all the help it can get when it comes to flavor. In poem 56 Stonehouse says he turned to yams when there was nothing else to eat.

145. In poem 15, Stonehouse says his hut has no gables. Apparently, this was why: the roof was round, like that of a yurt, with all the beams meeting at a central point. Buddhists say the universe contains a billion worlds, all of which were also able to fit inside Vimalakirti's hut in the sutra of the same name.

144   I repair my hoe and let my hut lean
        I farm clouds when I'm able and sleep when I'm tired
        yams turn ripe from summertime sun
        their flavor doesn't come from the stove

145   From outside my round pointed-roof hut
        who would guess at the space inside
        all the worlds in the universe are there
        with room to spare for a meditation cushion

草菴盤結長松下　面面軒窓盡豁開
目對青山終日坐　更無一事上心來

深秋時節雨霏霏　蘚葉層層印虎蹄
一夜西風吹不住　曉來黃葉與階齊

147.　The South China tiger, which is no longer seen in the wild, is much smaller than its Bengal or Siberian cousins. The Chinese associate the tiger with the wind, which rises when it roars. For more on the steps in front of Stonehouse's hut, see poem 163.

146   I built a thatch hut beneath tall pines
       windows open on every side
       all day I sit facing mountains
       nothing else comes to mind

147   Late autumn rain is all mist
       tiger tracks appear in the moss
       all last night the west wind blew
       by dawn the leaves were up to the steps

團團紅日上青山　竹屋柴門尚閉關
白髮老僧眠未起　勞生磨蟻正循環

山舍清幽絕點塵　心閒與世自相分
不知何處碧桃放　幽鳥街來遠竹門

149. Peach blossoms are reminiscent of T'ao Yuan-ming's story "Peach Blossom Spring," in which a fisherman once followed peach petals up a stream to an idyllic world.

148   When the red sun climbs above the blue mountains
the door of my hut is still closed
before the white-haired monk is up
ants are already making their rounds

149   My hut is so secluded it's beyond the reach of dust
my mind is so detached it's left the world behind
somewhere a peach tree is blooming
wild birds encircle my door with twigs

老來無事可干懷　竹榻高眠日枕斜
夢裏不知誰是我　覺來新月到梅花

禪餘高誦寒山偈　飯後濃煎穀雨茶
尚有閒情無着處　携籃過嶺採藤花

150. Obviously, a short and light sleep. The faint glow of the new moon is briefly visible just after sunset before it, too, follows the sun westward. As he tells us in poem 49, Stonehouse has a special sensitivity to moonlight on plum blossoms.

151. Cold Mountain, or Han-shan, lived during the second half of the eighth century and the first half of the ninth in the Tientai Mountains 250 kilometers south of Shanghai. The 300-odd poems he left behind have been translated into English by several people, including me. For chanting, Cold Mountain's poem 302 would have been a good choice: "The mountain I live on / nobody knows / here in the clouds / it's always deserted." Most varieties of tea benefit from frequent mist but not from heavy rain. The solar period known as grain-rain, *ku-yu* (穀雨), occurs in late April. Among the varieties for which the mountain is currently known, the most popular is *hsia-wu ts'ui-yu* (霞霧醉玉) (Redfog drunken-jade). "Vine flowers" refers, as in poem 142, to wisteria, the blossoms of which are a mountain delicacy and usually stir-fried.

150   Now that I'm old nothing disturbs me
       I'm asleep on my cot before the sun sets
       dreaming and wondering who I am
       until the new moon lights the plum blossoms

151   After meditation I chant a Cold Mountain poem
       after dinner I brew grain-rain tea
       and when some feeling lingers I can't express
       I take a basket across the ridge and gather vine flowers

僧因產業致差科
我有山田三畝半
官府勾追恥辱多
盡情回付與檀那

楮閣安爐種炭團
一冬煖活如何說
床鋪新薦被新綿
夢想不思兜率天

152. During various periods in Chinese history, monks were issued a small piece of land from which they supported themselves by farming or by renting it to others. During the Yuan dynasty, a special office was set up to handle monk affairs, and it was to this office that monks were required to apply. Ironically, Stonehouse was appointed the head of this office for the entire province in 1331 when he became abbot of Fuyuan Temple. However, the office was eliminated three years later.

153. Tushita Heaven is the highest of the heavens in the realm of desire and one in which all needs are satisfied and in which bodhisattvas reside prior to their final rebirth.

152   For property monks apply at an office
where bureaucratic snares and insults abound
I own a half acre of mountain land
I'm giving it back as alms when I die

153   I put mulberry wood in the stove to make charcoal
new cotton in my quilt a new mat on the bed
what can I say about staying warm all winter
I don't dream about Tushita Heaven

去年家火缺支持　家火今年用不虧
田裏多收三斗穀　門前添得一方池

白雲影裏尖頭屋　黃葉堆頭折腳鐺
漏笂籬撩無米飯　破砂盆擣爛生薑

154. The term *chia-huo* (home-fire) in the first line means "provisions," as it does in poem 87. Stonehouse had ponds he called Sky Lake at both his huts.

155. Stonehouse's round pointed-roof hut also appears in poem 145 and his three-legged pot in poem 140. Bowls with a coarse interior surface are still used in China for grating and extracting juice from rhizomes and roots.

154   Last year my food supply failed me
       this year I can't use it all
       I've harvested three bushels of grain too many
       and filled up the pond outside my door

155   A pointed-roof hut in the shade of the clouds
       a broken-legged pot on a pile of dry leaves
       a strainer with holes too big to strain rice
       and a cracked grating bowl for grating fresh ginger

修行豈得不成佛　水滴年深石也穿

不是頑皮鑽不破　惟人只欠自心堅

獨坐窮心寂杳冥　簡中無法可當情

西風吹盡擁門葉　留得空垞與月明

156. In "Choosing a Friend," the T'ang poet Meng Chiao wrote, "To be like the immortals / you need a mind as hard as iron."

156   How could someone who practices not become a buddha
if water drips long enough even rocks wear through
it's not true a thick skull can't be pierced
a person just needs a hard enough mind

157   I sit and meditate in the quiet and dark
where nothing comes to mind
I sweep in front when the west wind is done
I make a path for the moonlight

玉蝶梅花香滿樹　水池洗菜綠浮科
錦衣公子如知得　定是移家入薜蘿

逆順未嘗忘此道　窮通一味信前緣
是他了達虛空性　不動纖毫本自然

158   Jade-winged plum blossoms perfumed trees
pond-washed vegetables floating plants of green
if the silk-clad young lords knew about this
they would move into the wilds for sure

159   Good and bad fortune never lose their way
failure and success both depend on karma
realize distinctions are empty at heart
what doesn't move a hair is what's real

寒披荷葉衣裳煖　饑食松花餅餌香
不比世人營口體　奔南走北一生忙

160. Stonehouse's use of lotus leaves for clothing, especially cold-weather cloth-
ing, is somewhat facetious, as lotus leaves would be supple enough to wear only
during the summer. Stonehouse, however, mentions using them in poem 135.
He also mentions eating pine pollen in poem 12.

160   A lotus-leaf robe keeps me warm when I'm cold
pine-pollen cakes are a treat when I'm hungry
I'm not like those who worry about food and clothes
running north and south busy all their lives

新縫紙被煖烘烘
閒夢不知誰喚醒
黃葉堆頭火正紅
五更聽得下方鐘

新縫紙被烘來煖
聞得下方鐘鼓動
一覺安眠到五更
又添一日在浮生

161. The first version of this poem appears between poems 160 and 162 in all editions. The second version, however, appears only in later editions, such as the Ch'ing dynasty edition published by Taiwan's Hsinwenfeng Publishing Company, but in a different location: between poems 101 and 102. I've decided to include both. Unable to afford cloth, Stonehouse turned to a heavyweight paper (probably made from hemp or mulberry fiber) for the outer shell of his cotton-filled blanket, which here he heats up by hanging it above his hearth. Calling his blanket "newly sewn" suggests he has bought himself a new cover and sewn it up after inserting the cotton filling from the old blanket. In the third line of the second poem, the Ch'ing dynasty text has *shang-fang* (above) instead of *hsia-fang* (below), and is clearly a mistake. Most likely, the temple in question was Fuyuan Temple (not to be confused with the temple of the same name where Stonehouse served as abbot for seven years). The temple, though a shadow of its former size, is still there, outside the village of Yangshuwu at the northeast foot of Hsiamushan. During the Yuan dynasty, temple bells were rung at dusk, at midnight, and once more at dawn.

161   My newly sewn paper quilt is so warm
      and the pile of burning leaves is so red
      I wonder who will wake me from my dream
      then just before dawn I hear the bell down below

      I heat my newly sewn paper quilt
      and sleep all night until dawn
      when I hear the sound of a bell down below
      add one more day to this floating life

旋斫青柴逐把挑　擔頭防脫莫過腰
今朝未保得來日　且了寒爐一夜燒

今年難測是寒暄　一日陰晴變幾番
簷下紙窗乾又濕　門前石逕濕還乾

162. A late-spring cold wave finds Stonehouse short of wood and reduced to cutting saplings. The most common means of carrying things in China is still a bamboo pole placed over one or both shoulders and notched at both ends for ropes, to which loads can be attached and balanced. The trick is to keep the two loads level with one's waist. Stonehouse also mentions the fire pit in his earthen floor in poem 121. In North China, hermits use a k'ang, or oven-bed, to stay warm.

163. The Tienmu Mountains, of which Hsiamushan is a northern spur, receive a meter of rain annually, most of it falling between April and September.

162   I chop green wood and lift the pole
        I keep the load level with my waist
        what's here today won't last until tomorrow
        I fill my cold hearth and burn it all night

163   It's hard to say if the year has been hot or cold
        how many times does the sky change in a day
        my hut's paper windows are dry then they're wet
        the stone steps in front are wet then they're dry

峰頂團團盡是松　茅廬着在樹陰中
天風一陣來何處　吹起波濤響半空

黃羅直裰紫伽梨　　出入侯門得意時
爭似道人忘寵辱　　松針柳線補荷衣

164. The pines are gone. Now the summit is all bamboo and tea. Buddhists use
the metaphor of the ocean and its waves to explain our misperception of real-
ity, with its focus on the waves, which in this case would have been inspired by
those of nearby Taihu, China's third- or fourth-largest freshwater lake, depend-
ing on the time of year.

165. Monks chosen by the emperor to head the office in charge of monastic
affairs were allowed to wear the imperial colors of purple and yellow and were
given special access to imperial quarters.

164   Surrounding the summit is nothing but pines
and my thatch hut is set in their shade
where does that gust of wind come from
stirring up waves echoing across the sky

165   Sewing purple robes with fine yellow silk
they achieve their goals through back doors
no match for a hermit beyond praise and blame
with willow floss and pine needle mending lotus-leaf clothes

春歸暑退一秋涼　日暮如梭夜漸長
盡把工夫閒雜話　幾曾回首暫思量

我見時人日夜忙　廣營屋宅置田莊
到頭一事將不去　獨有骷髏葬北邙

166. The shuttle of a loom is meant.

167. Peimang is the name of a long, low ridge of hills between the ancient city of Loyang and the Yellow River. It was used as a cemetery by the wealthy and powerful as early as three thousand years ago. A popular saying in ancient times went: "To be born in Hangchou / to be buried on Peimang."

166   Spring is gone summer is gone and autumn is cool
the days are like a shuttle and the nights are getting long
people fill their time with idle talk and chatter
how often do they stop and think

167   The people I meet are busy night and day
enlarging their houses or clearing more land
until that day none can escape
when all they own are bones on Peimang

箇箇聞知有死生　聞知何不早修行
堂堂大道無人到　開眼明明入火坑

盡說修行不在遲　今生還有後生期
三塗一報五千劫　出得頭來是幾時

168. By "cultivate," Stonehouse means to clear the mind of delusion through meditation and other practices. Buddhists believed there were a number of hot hells as well as cold hells.

169. A kalpa is the length of time between a world's creation and its destruction. In the third line, "below" refers to the three lower realms of rebirth: not only as a denizen of one of the hells but also as a hungry ghost or as some kind of nonhuman creature.

168 People all know about death and rebirth
     why then don't they cultivate
     instead of walking the wide-open Way
     they enter the fiery pit clear-eyed

169 People all say there is time to cultivate
     if not now there is still next year
     but headed for five thousand kalpas below
     they won't be back anytime soon

山名霞幕泉天湖
山頭有塊臺盤石
更有天湖一泉水
就泉結屋擬終老
外面規模似狹窄
碧紗如煙隔金像
蒲團禪椅列左右
瓷甖土種吉祥草
飯香粥滑山田米
得失是非都放卻
有時把柄白塵拂
懶舉西來祖意說

卜居記得壬子初
宛如出水青芙蕖
先天至今何曾枯
田地一點紅塵無
中間取用能寬舒
雕盤沉水凌天衢
香鐘雲板鳴朝晡
石盤水養龍池蒲
瓜甜菜嫩家園蔬
經行坐臥無相拘
有時持串烏木珠
甚東魯詩書

170. Poems 170–184 are missing from later editions but present in all three Ming dynasty copies of the *Mountain Poems*. Hsiamushan, according to maps found in old gazetteers for the Huchou area, refers to the southern summit, while Hsiawushan refers to the northern one. The Yuan dynasty's reign period known as Imperial Celebration (Huangching [皇慶]) began in 1312 and ended in 1313. The flat lotus-shaped rock is still there, just up the slope from where Stonehouse built his first hut. No doubt the rock was a good place to meditate. Good-luck grass, or *Reineckia carnea*, is a member of the lily family. Its association with good fortune and its ability to flourish indoors have made it a common sight in shrine halls. Dragon-pool rushes are those that grow near waterfalls. For the whisk, see my note to poem 56. Beads are used to count repetitions during chanting. A meditation chair is much wider than a normal chair so that it can accommodate someone sitting in the lotus position with their legs crossed. Meditation periods were marked by lighting a stick of incense of a set length and ringing a small handbell. A bronze cloud-shaped gong was also used in Buddhist temples to announce periods of assembly. I'm not sure what Stonehouse is doing with one, unless he just likes making music. Or perhaps he liked to use it

170   To Redcurtain Mountain and Sky Lake Spring
I moved at the start of Imperial Celebration
to a flat-topped rock near the summit
like a blue lotus rising from a pool
and a spring I call Sky Lake
flowing without cease since the world began
here I cleared a field of worldly dust
and built a hut to live out my old age
from outside it might look small
but inside there is room for all my things
a gilt statue veiled by emerald silk
a carved bowl whose water reaches the vault of heaven
a straw cushion and meditation chair
incense bell and gong to mark the dusk and dawn
I planted good-luck grass in a porcelain pot
and dragon-pool rushes in a basin of stone
mountain-grown rice is fragrant and smooth
vegetables from my garden are tender and sweet
I've abandoned right and wrong success and failure
I don't care how I walk or sit or lie down
sometimes I pick up my deer-tail whisk
sometimes I finger my black wooden beads
sometimes I feel like dancing
sometimes I sit like a dunce
too lazy to explain why Bodhidharma came east
much less the poetry or annals of Lu

自亦不知是凡是聖　他豈能識是牛是驢

客來未暇陪說話　拾枯先去燒茶爐

紅香旖旎春花開敷　清陰繁茂夏木翳如

巖桂風前喚回山谷　梅花雪裏清殺林逋

人間無此真樂　山中有甚凶虞

也不樂他輕輿高蓋　也不樂他率眾匡徒

也不樂他西方極樂　也不樂他天上淨居

心下常無不足　目前觸事有餘

夜籟合樂曉天　昇鳥戲魚翻躍

好鳥相呼　路通玄以幽遠境

超世而清虛　騷人盡思吟不成句

丹青極巧畫不成圖　獨有淵明可起予解道

吾亦愛吾廬　山中居沒閒時

無人會惟自知　遠山驅竹筧寒水

to mark dusk and dawn. Bodhidharma is credited with bringing Zen to China, and by the seventh century Zen masters were using the reason for his arrival as the subject of meditation. The *Book of Poetry* and the *Spring and Autumn Annals of Lu* are among the works all scholars and would-be officials were expected to know by heart. Both were attributed to Confucius, who spent most of his life in the state of Lu (in Shantung province). Shan-ku was the pen name of Huang T'ing-chien (黃庭堅 1045–1105), whose poetry immortalized cassia flowers. Lin Pu (967–1028), or Lin Ho-ching, did the same with plum flowers. Achieving rebirth in the Western Paradise of Amita Buddha was the goal of Pure Land Buddhists. Sloughing off this mortal coil and ascending to a pure realm in the heavens was the goal of certain Taoist practitioners. The "crow" refers to the sun, on which lives a three-legged crow. One day Chuang-tzu said the fish he saw below a bridge were happy, and his companion questioned his ability to know what the fish knew, to which Chuang-tzu replied, "How do you know I don't know?" (*Chuangtzu*: 17). Mount Sumeru is at the center of every world and as many miles high as there are grains of sand in the Ganges. Dirt includes the dust of sensation, but it also includes emptiness as well.

I don't know if I'm a fool or a sage
or if others are oxen or donkeys
when a guest arrives there's no time to chat
I gather dry wood and light the tea stove
perfumed red pennants unfold in spring
the foliage of summer shade is brief
a gust of wild cassia calls Shan-ku to mind
plum blossoms in the snow purified Lin Pu
true joys like these aren't found in town
in the mountains you won't find evil
I don't want a fancy carriage
I don't want a flock of disciples
I don't want a Western Paradise
I don't want a pure celestial abode
my mind has enough to think about
my eyes have plenty to see
the music of the wind at night
the crow on the wing at dawn
fish swim and jump for joy
birds call back and forth with delight
on the road to the dark and distant
in the realm of transcendence and void
inspired poets are speechless
master artists can't paint
only Yuan-ming could play with the Tao
like him I love my hut
but in the mountains there's no leisure
and yet I've learned what others don't know
how to channel a spring around a slope with bamboo

擊石取火延朝炊
香粳旋舂柴旋斫
砂鍋未滾涎先垂
開畬未及種紫芋
鉏地更要栽黃萁
白日不得手腳住
黃昏未到神思疲
歸來洗足上床睡
困重不知山月移
隔林幽鳥忽喚醒
一團紅日懸松枝
今日明日也如是
來年後年還如斯
春草離離夏木葳
秋雲片片冬雪霏
虛空落地須彌碎
三世如來脫垢衣

how to start the morning fire with a rock
how to pound mountain rice and chop wood
before the pot boils I drool
on uncleared land I plant taro
and beans where I've managed to hoe
I don't stop moving all day
before the sun sets I'm exhausted
back home I wash my feet and lie down
too tired to notice the phases of the moon
birds from the next forest over wake me up
along with the sun's red disk through the pines
today and tomorrow are the same
last year and next year no change
in spring plants sprout in summer they flourish
in autumn clouds gather in winter it snows
when the sky falls to earth Sumeru shatters
buddhas take off their dirty clothes

晴明無事登霞峰
伸眉望極開心胸
太湖萬頃白瀲灩
洞庭兩點青濛茸
初疑仙子始綰角
碧紗帽子參差籠
又疑天女來獻花
玉盤捧出雙芙蓉
明知此境俱幻妄
對此悠然心未終
徘徊不忍便歸去
夕陽又轉山頭松

171. Stonehouse begins this poem standing at the summit of Hsiawushan (the northern part of the mountain) looking northeast across Lake Taihu. Covering more than 2,500 square kilometers, Taihu is China's third- or fourth-largest freshwater lake, depending on the season. On the northeast corner of the lake and about 50 kilometers from where Stonehouse was standing are an island and an adjacent peninsula known as West Tungting and East Tungting, respectively. Both are about 100 square kilometers in area and 300 meters in elevation. Stonehouse's hometown of Changshu was another 70 kilometers past these two "emerald buds."

171 A clear sky and nothing planned I climbed Hsia Summit
   I opened my heart and gazed into the distance
   the shimmering white expanse of Taihu
   and the two emerald buds of Tungting
   I imagined at first were a young immortal's topknots
   and silk cap with uneven sides
   then a deity's offering of flowers
   two lotuses rising from a basin of jade
   such scenes I knew were fantasies
   but my mind wandered on without stop
   until I couldn't bear it and went back down
   at sunset I turned again toward the summit pines

乾鵲傍簷鳴鵲喳
西菴道者來送果
吉凶占相既有驗
道人若有此見解
懶融一見四祖後

烏鴉遠屋聲鴉啞
東鄰稚子去偷瓜
罪福果報應無差
青銅鏡面生痕瑕
百鳥更不來御花

172. The Chinese consider magpies good luck and crows bad luck. The third couplet reads as if it were a quote. If so, I'm at a loss as to its source. Chinese mirrors were made of bronze and were small, convex, and polished on one side. Tao-hsin was the Fourth Patriarch of Zen, and his disciple Fa-yung was the founder of the Oxhead Zen lineage. Fa-yung was called lazy because he never stood up or bowed to greet visitors. One day while Tao-hsin was in Nan-ching, he saw birds flocking around a mountain to the south. When he went to investigate, he found Fa-yung meditating and the birds dropping flowers on him. But he also saw wolf tracks and tiger tracks and feigned fright at such a sight. Seeing this reaction, Fa-yung said, "There is still that in you?" Tao-hsin responded by drawing the character for "buddha" in the dirt in front of Fa-yung. When Fa-yung expressed embarrassment, Tao-hsin said, "There is still that in you?" After this meeting, the birds and wild animals stopped visiting Fa-yung (*Chuantenglu*: 4). Hence, despite his attainments, Fa-yung had yet to overcome his attainments.

172   Magpies talk magpie outside my hut
crows talk crow circling my roof
a hermit to the west brings me fruits
a boy to the east steals my melons
we see the signs of blessing and disaster
but we shouldn't separate good and bad fortune
followers of the Way who cling to such views
see defects on a polished mirror
after Lazy Yung met Tao-hsin
birds stopped bringing him flowers

林木長新葉
深草沒塵跡
自耕復自種
好雨及時來
遊目周宇宙
既善解空理

遠屋清陰多
隔山聽樵歌
側笠披青簑
活我新栽禾
物物皆消磨
不樂還如何

寒山曾有言
我亦曾有言
秋月非不明
安得如我心
有問心如何

吾心似秋月
吾心勝秋月
有圓復有缺
圓明常皎潔
教我如何說

173. Most farmers in the Yangtze and West River watersheds in China wear hats made of a framework of bamboo strips and an outer covering of bamboo leaves. Until recently, the standard raincoat in South China consisted of layers of palm tree bark or coconut husk fiber. The summer monsoon, which the Chinese call "plum rains," normally arrives mid-June along with the first plums and is crucial for transplanting rice sprouts. The first of the Buddha's Four Noble Truths is "All is sorrow," which itself is based on the realization that all things are impermanent and thus empty of self-existence.

174. Among the more than three hundred poems attributed to Cold Mountain, poem 5 is one of my favorites and one of Stonehouse's, too: "My mind is like the autumn moon / clear and bright in a pool of jade / nothing can compare / what more can I say."

173   The trees in the forest grow new leaves
surrounding my hut with more cool shade
tall grass hides my tracks
over the ridge I hear a woodcutter sing
I plow and I plant
my tree-bark coat and leaf hat askew
the rain comes in time
my rice sprouts are saved
I've scanned the whole world
everything fades
having understood emptiness
what do I do about sorrow

174   Cold Mountain has a line
My mind is like the autumn moon
I have a line of my own
my mind outshines the autumn moon
not that the autumn moon isn't bright
but once it's full it fades
how unlike my mind
forever full and bright
as for what the mind is like
what more can I say

月來照我門
勸君石上坐
玄鬢化為雪
萬事草頭露

風來吹我襟
聽我山中吟
朝光成夕陰
豈得長如今

飯飽拂石睡
靄靄盂夏景
俯仰翫時物
只此是真樂

睡足起閒行
新樹鳴黃鶯
散誕暢吟情
何必求虛名

175. Loosening the lapels of one's robe and exposing one's chest is a metaphor for revealing one's innermost feelings. The penultimate line recalls an ancient folk song known as "Dew on the Leek": "Dew on the leek / how quickly it dries / it dries and tomorrow falls once again / but when do we return from the grave?"

176. Stonehouse is probably referring to the flat-topped boulder just uphill from his first hut, the one farmers nowadays call "chess-playing rock." In the *Great Learning* (3.2), Confucius is reported to have said, "The *Book of Odes* says, 'The twittering oriole / rests at the top of the hill.' When it rests, it knows where to rest. Is it possible man is not equal to this bird?" In the background here is this story at the end of chapter 17 in *Chuangtzu:* "One day when Chuang-tzu and Hui-tzu were walking across the Hao River Bridge, Chuang-tzu said, 'See the fish rising and swimming so gracefully. This is what makes fish happy.' Hui-tzu said, 'You're not a fish. How do you know what makes a fish happy?' Chuang-tzu replied, 'You're not me. How do you know I don't know what makes a fish happy?' Hui-tzu said, 'I'm not you, so I certainly don't know. But you're certainly not a fish. Hence, you can't know what makes a fish happy.' Chuang-tzu said, 'Let's go back to the beginning. You asked how I knew what makes a fish happy. So when you asked, you already knew that I knew.'" In the last line, the phrase *empty names* usually refers to fame, but here it also refers to illusory goals to which we give names, goals such as buddhahood.

175   The moon lights up my door
       the wind blows open my robe
       sit down on a rock my friend
       hear my mountain song
       black hair turns to snow
       dawn light to evening shade
       everything is dew on the grass
       nothing stays the same

176   After a meal I dust off a boulder and sleep
       and after I sleep I go for a walk
       on a cloudy late summer day
       an oriole sings from a sapling
       enjoying the season while it can
       joyfully singing out its heart
       true happiness is right here
       why chase empty names

小不讀佛書　大不識玄旨
焉知百萬門　只在方寸裡
終日恣貪嗔　幾時念生死
一朝老病來　懊惱亦徒爾

種豆兩三畦　離離覆原上
不知陽和功　惟言土力壯
老兔伏崖根　心心欲希望
果能息汝貪　我寧不食醬

177. Since ancient times, education in China began with memorization. Only later were the memorized texts explained. The sutras of the Buddha say there are a million doors to the truth but you only need to walk through one of them. Buddhists often refer to the mind as the "square inch."

177   If you don't read sutras when you're young
      you won't know what they mean when you're older
      you won't know a million doorways
      are all inside the square inch of your mind
      indulging all day in desire and hate
      how often do you think about life and death
      one day illness or old age will surprise you
      remorse then will be too late

178   I planted a few hills of beans
      their tendrils now cover the summit
      forgetting the sunshine and sweat
      I say it's all in the soil
      an old rabbit crouches at the base of the cliff
      fantasies filling its thoughts
      if it would give up its desires
      I would give up soy sauce

山中一雨滋
原上百物好
手種三畝薯
亦可延昏早
咄哉世間人
名利常關抱
頭上雪紛紛
胸中塵浩浩

結屋荒山巔
隨緣度朝夕
賣柴糴米歸
羹粥做飯喫
雖是勞形骸
且免當戶役
說妙與談玄
簡卻曉不得

179. As noted elsewhere, the yam was one of Stonehouse's least favorite food options—more of a starvation food. An acre of them would have meant an awful lot of depressing meals. As elsewhere, "dust" refers to sensation and desire for sensation.

180. In ancient China, the government required every household with able-bodied males to provide a certain number of days' labor on government construction projects or service in the local militia or army. But since monks were no longer members of a household, they were exempt from such forms of labor. The "dark and distant" refer to Taoist and Buddhist profundities.

179 Whenever the mountain enjoys a good rain
   everything flourishes here on the summit
   planting an acre of yams
   can wait for another time
   people in the world alas
   keep thinking of fortune and fame
   heads aswirl with snow
   hearts awash with dust

180 I built my hut on a desolate ridge
   and pass my days in karma's wake
   I sell firewood to buy grain
   and live on porridge and rice
   although I wear myself out
   at least I avoid corvée
   but talking about the dark and distant
   that is something I can't do

放下全放下
動念即成魔
飲啄但隨緣
執法去修行

佛也莫要做
開口便招禍
只麼閒閒過
牽牛來拽磨

破屋三兩椽
雲散天宇清
世界空裡花
日落山風寒

住在千峰上
放目聊四望
起滅皆虛妄
閉門燒火向

181. Buddhists recognize an infinite number of demons, or maras, one for every thought, word, and deed. The purpose of these demons is to obstruct us from understanding the true nature of reality. *Dharma* is the Buddhist word for what is held to be real, especially the Buddha's teaching. As early as the T'ang and Sung dynasties, Chinese monks used the ox as a metaphor for the untamed mind. Among the most famous examples of this usage was the series of oxherding pictures and accompanying verses by P'u Ming (普明) describing the stages of Zen training.

182. During the Yuan dynasty, structures were measured by the number of rafters used in their construction, and taxation of householders was assessed on this basis—though without much success. By Stonehouse's time, when the owners of a building paid taxes on what they reported as being "three rafters" (三椽), the actual width had expanded from three feet to nine feet. Hence, they paid only one-third of the taxes they should have. In poem 97, Stonehouse says his hut was two or three mats wide, a mat being equivalent to three feet. And in poem 129, he says his hut wasn't quite ten feet on a side. By "a thousand peaks," Stonehouse is referring to the dozen or so smaller hills around Hsiamushan.

181   Letting go means letting everything go
        buddhahood has to go too
        each thought becomes a demon
        each word invites more trouble
        survive instead on what karma brings
        pass your days in freedom
        make the Dharma your practice
        lead your ox to the mill

182   My broken-down hut isn't three rafters wide
        perched above a thousand peaks
        when clouds unveil an azure sky
        I let my eyes roam the four horizons
        the world is a flower in space
        its bloom and decay are delusions
        when the sun goes down and the wind turns cold
        I close my door and face the fire

結屋霞峰頭
山田六七坵
開池放月來
老子少機關

耕鈕供日課
道人二兩箇
賣柴糴米過
家私都說破

兩箇窮道人
開得一坵田
煮粥儘有餘
也勝利名人

三間弊漏屋
收得半擔穀
做飯却不足
奔南又走北

183. The term *chia-ssu* (patrimony, inherited possessions) in the last line also appears in poem 37.

184. Stonehouse shared the mountain with others, especially during his second residence on the mountain. No doubt, his neighbors included the monk Chih-jou, whose name appears as the editor of his *Mountain Poems* as well as his *Gathas* and *Zen Talks*.

183 I built my hut on top of Hsia Summit
 plowing and hoeing make up my day
 half a dozen terraced fields
 two or three hermit neighbors
 I made a pond for the moon
 and sell wood to buy grain
 an old man with few schemes
 I've told you all that I own

184 A couple of impoverished monks
 living in broken-down huts
 clearing terraced fields
 we harvest a basket of chaff
 enough to make porridge
 but not enough for a meal
 still we outdo the rich and famous
 racing north and hurrying south

Red Pine, Finn Wilcox, and Steve Johnson at the site of Stonehouse's first hut, 1991.

Bill Porter's translations have been honored with a number of awards, including two NEA translation fellowships, a PEN translation award, the inaugural Asian Literature Award of the American Literary Translators Association, and more recently a Guggenheim Fellowship, which he received to support work on a book based on a pilgrimage to the graves and homes of over thirty of China's greatest poets of the past.

Poetry is vital to language and living. Since 1972, Copper Canyon Press has published extraordinary poetry from around the world to engage the imaginations and intellects of readers, writers, booksellers, librarians, teachers, students, and donors.

WE ARE GRATEFUL FOR THE MAJOR SUPPORT PROVIDED BY:

THE PAUL G. ALLEN
FAMILY FOUNDATION

Lannan

THE MAURER FAMILY
FOUNDATION

ART WORKS.
National
Endowment
for the Arts
arts.gov

WASHINGTON STATE
ARTS COMMISSION

Anonymous
John Branch
Diana and Jay Broze
Beroz Ferrell & The Point, LLC
Janet and Les Cox
Mimi Gardner Gates
Gull Industries, Inc.
on behalf of William and Ruth True
Mark Hamilton and Suzie Rapp
Carolyn and Robert Hedin
Steven Myron Holl
Lakeside Industries, Inc.
on behalf of Jeanne Marie Lee
Maureen Lee and Mark Busto
Brice Marden
H. Stewart Parker
Penny and Jerry Peabody
John Phillips and Anne O'Donnell
Joseph C. Roberts
Cynthia Lovelace Sears and Frank Buxton
The Seattle Foundation
Dan Waggoner
Charles and Barbara Wright
The dedicated interns and faithful
volunteers of Copper Canyon Press

To learn more about underwriting Copper Canyon Press titles,
please call 360-385-4925 ext. 103

The Chinese character for poetry is made up of two parts: "word" and "temple." It also serves as pressmark for Copper Canyon Press.

This book is set in Minion, designed for digital composition by Robert Slimbach in 1989. Minion is a neohumanist face, a contemporary typeface retaining elements of the pen-drawn letterforms developed during the Renaissance. Display type is set in Perpetua Titling, designed by Eric Gill. Chinese set by Pristine in STKaiti. Book design and composition by VJB/Scribe. Printed on archival-quality paper.